This book belongs to _____

confirmed on_____

at _____

Signature of priest _____

Signature of bishop _____

Faith
CONFIRMED

Preparing for
confirmation

PETER JACKSON
and
CHRIS WRIGHT

North American edition, published by Forward Movement 2019

Originally printed by Society for Promoting Christian Knowledge, www.spckpublishing.co.uk

Reprinted six times
Second edition published 2013

The authors and the publisher would like to express their gratitude to Jeffrey John and Bishop David Stancliffe, and others at Affirming Catholicism, for their help in bringing this project to fruition.

Scripture quotations are from the New Revised Standard Version of the Bible, copyright © 1989 National Council of the Churches of Christ in the United States of America. Used by permission. All rights reserved.

Psalm passages are from the Psalter of *The Book of Common Prayer*.

For photo acknowledgments, see page 129

ISBN: 978-0-88028-467-7

Printed in USA

www.forwardmovement.org

Faith
CONFIRMED

Preparing for confirmation

PETER JACKSON
and
CHRIS WRIGHT

Forward Movement

Cincinnati, Ohio

Contents

CONTENTS

About this book

In the introduction to this book, we compare confirming our faith in Jesus to deciding to travel through life with a really accurate map. Each chapter of the book forms part of the map. When you look at a map, you have to find your bearings; similarly, it's best to glance through the layout of each chapter before you read it properly.

Each chapter begins with a story or stories and pictures that are designed to provide a bridge between ideas and experiences already familiar to you and the Christian beliefs you will need to find out about. Further factual information is provided in boxes headed "Christian beliefs." You can use these for reference or to explore the ideas in greater detail. There are more stories and explanations later in the chapter to deepen your understanding.

Each chapter (except Chapter 11) concludes with three standard sections:

Thinking it through provides you with some questions to ask yourself. They can also be used to open up group discussion. To answer them, you can turn back and look through the chapter but you can also draw on your own experience.

Bible study can be used on your own or in a group. It should help you to understand how Christian beliefs are rooted in the Bible.

For prayer and reflection provides you with a prayer that you may use privately or say together in a group. You may also like to make up your own prayers reflecting what you have learned from the chapter, and you will find some suggestions for prayer topics at the end of each chapter.

To those leading groups preparing for confirmation

We have aimed in writing this book to make a simple, accessible, and attractive presentation of what Episcopalians believe. Inevitably, individuals may quibble over details and points of emphasis but we believe that a coherent exposition of Episcopal belief is possible and desirable if we are effectively to draw people into active, thoughtful, and committed membership of the Church.

The main practical principle behind the writing of this book is that people need bridges between their own experience and Christian concepts. These are best provided by pictures and stories. Once contact has been made between the reader and the main Christian concept, the group leader can then choose from a wide variety of material.

Preparation for confirmation introduces us to the Christian "map" for our journey through life.

already gone some way on their personal Christian journey and wish simply to know more about the Christian faith. Experience has shown that it is useful to readers of all ages. We hope that readers will read some or all of the book on their own.

Finally, our own experience has led us to believe that the "For prayer and reflection" sections can be particularly rewarding. Often, when a group or individuals compose their own prayers, they give personal expression to the Christian beliefs they have studied. This process is another way to engage the hearts and the minds.

A note on this edition

Originally published in England, this book has been updated for the Episcopal Church. While some small differences exist between the Church of England and the Episcopal Church, the fundamental principles of confirmation and commiting one's life to Christ are, thankfully, the same.

Each chapter is laid out in much the same way, in sections, as described above. The time available and the age and ability of your group will affect how much coverage you can allocate to each section.

The book has been designed very much to be the personal possession of each reader. It will be used particularly by those preparing for confirmation, but it will also be valuable to those who have

Introduction

When we confirm something, we say yes. At confirmation we say yes to Jesus' call to follow him on our journey through life. We confirm our faith in him. Parents and godparents will usually have said yes for us when we were babies and unable to speak for ourselves at baptism, but confirmation gives *us* the chance to say yes.

We have all had the experience of getting lost. This can happen because we have no map or an inadequate one, or because our smartphone or other mapping service isn't working properly. Confirming our faith in Jesus is like deciding to travel through life with a really accurate map. This book aims to help you become familiar with the main features of the "Christian map."

On the contents page, you will find its landmarks. Some of these will be familiar to you and others new. Although it will make sense if you read the book on your own, we hope you will share it with others. Just as planning a journey is more fun when you discuss it with others, so Christianity makes more sense when it's experienced and lived with other people. We hope also that you will refer back to this guide after your confirmation. On long journeys, we have to keep on checking our directions. To carry the "journey" picture a bit further: why not see confirmation as a time to take stock of where you have come from and seek God's help in preparing for what lies ahead?

Chapter 1
GOD

Do you believe in God the Father?
I believe in God, the Father almighty,
creator of heaven and earth.

—*The Book of Common Prayer*, p. 304

If you are reading this book, you may already believe in God, or you may be unsure about believing but curious about exploring belief. But where did this belief or curiosity about belief come from?

Maybe you were brought up to believe in God by your parents, or you have seen God at work in people you respect and look up to. Maybe you or someone close to you has been very ill or has died and this has made you wonder about what life means and whether God plays a part in your life. Maybe you started to believe in or wondered about God as the creator of the world as you looked around at the order and beauty of the natural world. Maybe you began to believe in God or to be curious about God from reading the Bible. Or maybe you started to feel that there was an unseen hand guiding your life, that coincidences were signs of God, present through the circumstances and the people you met.

Some people, like David's parents, started to believe in God as a result of a crisis. When their son died, his family was devastated. They felt their world had come to an end. All their hopes had been destroyed. Their life became one long nightmare. However, in their despair, their son's death became a religious experience for the family—they woke up to what was important in life, turned to God, began reading the Bible and going to church, and within a year were confirmed in the church.

How do we know God?

God is waiting to enter into a loving relationship with each of us. God reveals this in a number of ways.

Through the Bible and the Church

The Bible is our main source for understanding how God has acted and how Jesus came into the world to save us.

As we will see in Chapter 8, the Bible was produced over a very long period. Therefore, it provides us with a unique record of how countless generations experienced God's presence and actions and bore witness to them.

Christians believe that God inspired the different authors of the books of the Bible to write them so that the revelation of Godself should be kept alive for later generations.

The Church has done this by translating and copying the Bible but also by teaching about the Bible and applying it afresh to new circumstances. It is a living book kept alive by the living community of the Church.

That is one of the reasons why we have provided suggestions for Bible study in this book. We cannot hear the Bible as the living Word of God unless we study it and give it time to speak to us.

Through God's creation

Have you ever felt a sense of awe and wonder at nature—maybe standing under a waterfall or on top of a mountain or being caught in a thunderstorm? Many people have felt God's powerful presence in the world God created. Its beauty and majesty have revealed God's beauty and majesty to them.

Through experiences in life

What does it mean to say a person has a conscience? Have you ever felt your conscience telling you to do something or to stop doing something? Where does your sense of right and wrong come from?

Christians believe that God speaks to people through their conscience. They can develop their conscience by learning about what the Bible and the Church's tradition teach.

Sometimes we have experiences which make us stand back and ask, "Where did that come from?"

God speaks to us through our everyday life—through the people we meet and the things that happen. Sometimes people dismiss these experiences as coincidences and ignore the fact that God may be speaking to us through them. To respond

Many people say they find God in nature. Does this picture make you think of God? What images in your life remind you of God?

well to these experiences, we need to give ourselves time to reflect on their meaning —we need time to discern.

Sometimes God speaks to people in an unmistakable way. Such people say that they have experienced a conversion in which their lives have been shaken up and turned around. However, for other people, their conversion is very gradual and may take many years—it is a slow realization that their values and attitudes are changing and being brought more in line with God's wishes for them.

Through prayer

God is a personal God. We believe that God speaks to us through prayer. As with any relationship we need to spend time together—to talk and listen to each other. This is what prayer is—a time of talking and listening to God. Without prayer the relationship would become dry. Prayer is the way we communicate with God.

What is going on in this photograph? How can you tell? If you were able to hear this person speak, you would hear only one side of the conversation. In what sense does the person hear the other side of the conversation?

Christian beliefs about God

• **God created the universe.** God is involved with the world and is in constant interaction with it. The story of the Bible is the story of salvation history, of how God interacts with history to save his people.

• **God is unique.**

– *God is everywhere* (omnipresent). The Bible teaches that there is nowhere outside his presence: "Where can I go then from your Spirit? Where can I flee from your presence?" (Psalm 139:6).

– *God is all-powerful* (omnipotent). God will judge all people and will overcome all forces of darkness in the world: "I know that you can do all things, and that no purpose of yours can be thwarted" (Job 42:2).

– *God knows everything* (omniscient). God can see the past, present and future. God fully understands people's needs and secret thoughts: "O LORD, you have searched me out and known me. You know my sitting down and my rising up; you discern my thoughts from afar. Indeed, there is not a word on my lips, but you O LORD, know it altogether" (Psalm 139:1-3).

– *God is above space and time* (eternal, unchanging). God has always existed and owes his existence to no one: "Thus says the LORD, the King of Israel, and his Redeemer, the LORD of hosts: I am the first and I am the last; besides me there is no god" (Isaiah 44:6).

• **God is holy and wants people to be holy.** The word "holy" describes God's perfect nature. God sets holy standards for people to live up to—like the Ten Commandments.

• **God has different attributes.** The Bible uses a number of word pictures to describe different attributes of God. God is likened to a shepherd: "The LORD is my shepherd, I shall not be in want" (Psalm 23:1); a rock, shield, and fortress: "O LORD my stronghold, my crag, and my haven. My God, my rock in whom I put my trust, my shield, the horn of my salvation, and my praise" (Psalm 18:1-2); a judge: "for the LORD is a God of knowledge, and by him actions are weighed" (1 Samuel 2:3); a king: "Who would not fear you, O King of the nations?...In all their kingdoms there is no one like you" (Jeremiah 10:7).

• **God reveals Godself in a number of ways.** This includes through God's actions in history: "Listen to me in silence...Who has roused a victor from the east, summoned him to his service? He delivers up nations to him, and tramples kings under foot; he makes them like dust with his sword, like driven stubble with his bow...Who has performed and done this, calling the generations from the beginning? I, the LORD, am first, and will be with the last" (Isaiah 41:1-4).

− *God reveals Godself in the Bible:* "You must understand this, that no prophecy of scripture is a matter of one's own interpretation, because no prophecy ever came by human will, but men and women moved by the Holy Spirit spoke from God" (2 Peter 1:20-21).

− *God reveals Godself through creation:* "The heavens declare the glory of God" (Psalm 19:1); "Ever since the creation of the world his eternal power and divine nature, invisible though they are, have been understood and seen through the things he has made" (Romans 1:20).

− *God revealed Godself fully in Jesus.* Jesus' life and teaching showed people what God was truly like. Jesus is sometimes described as the human window into God. Jesus said: "Whoever has seen me has seen the Father" (John 14:9).

• **God makes covenants (agreements) with people.** God makes promises to humanity, and although people break their promises, God is faithful in keeping God's promises. God is like the loving and forgiving father in the parable of the Prodigal Son: "But while he was still far off, his father saw him and was filled with compassion; he ran and put his arms around him and kissed him" (Luke 15:20). God is pictured in Hosea as a generous lover: in spite of people disobeying God and the laws, God still loves them.

• **God is not just male.** Although God is often referred to in the masculine, many Christians do not believe in a male concept of God. In the Bible God is likened both to a father: "The LORD your God...will fight for you, just as he did for you in Egypt before your very eyes, and in the wilderness, where you saw how the LORD your God carried you, just as one carries a child" (Deuteronomy 1:30-31); and a mother: "Can a woman forget her nursing-child, or show no compassion for the child of her womb? Even these may forget, yet I will not forget you" (Isaiah 49:15).

• **God is one being but is also three persons:** Father, Son and Holy Spirit, who are all equally God. This three-in-one God is known as the Trinity.

• **We can know God through faith,** by putting our trust in God, even though God is greater than words can describe or than we can imagine.

What kind of God do we believe in?

God is holy

Light is a symbol often used to describe God. It points to God's glory or holiness. The word "holy" describes God's perfect nature. Christians believe that God made people and God wants them to be holy too. This is why God has said that there is a right way to live. God has set holy standards, not to make life miserable and hard but to allow love and happiness to grow. The Christian way of life is called holiness. A Christian is made whole by knowing God.

God is Trinity

We believe in one God revealed in three distinct persons: as the Father who created the world, as the Son who came to bring forgiveness and rescue humanity, and as the Holy Spirit who is the Spirit of God filling people with love, joy, and peace and making them more like Christ. Christians refer to the three-in-one nature of God as the Trinity.

We find a very early reference to the three-in-one nature of God in the last words of Paul's second letter to the Corinthian Church: "The grace of the Lord Jesus Christ, the love of God, and the communion of the Holy Spirit be with all of you" (2 Corinthians 13:13).

In our everyday experience we know of different things that at the same time can be one. For example, water, ice, and steam are different states of the chemical H_2O. The same person can be a mother, a cousin, and a sister all at the same time.

But what do we mean when we say that God is One in three persons? The Latin word *persona* (way of being) referred to a Roman actor's mask, which changed with each different role. The belief in God as Trinity is saying "we believe in one God who exists and works in three ways." Christians experience God in three distinct personal ways.

The doctrine of the Trinity means that God can be likened to a communion of persons, eternally linked by love. Father, Son and Holy Spirit are eternally united by love, and Scripture says that "God is love" (1 John 4:8). That is why when we truly love others, then we are most like God.

A creator God

James Weldon Johnson, an American author and early civil rights activist, describes the creation of the world in a poem:

> *And God stepped out on space,*
> *And he looked around and said:*
> *I'm lonely –*
> *I'll make me a world . . .*
>
> From "The Creation"[1]

We believe that God created the world out of love and that evidence of this creating can be found in the beauty and detail of nature.

But what about suffering?

How are the three persons of the Trinity represented here? What message do you think the painter El Greco is trying to give?

God is the sea in which I swim, the atmosphere in which I breathe, the reality in which I move. I cannot find the tiniest thing which does not speak to me of Him, which is not somehow His image, His message, His call, His smile.

Carlo Carretto, *Love is for Living*[2]

The existence of suffering in the world is the greatest obstacle preventing people from believing in a loving God. How do you explain belief in God in the face of so much suffering?

One partial way to understand the problem of suffering is to recognize that a lot of it can be traced to the fact that people have rebelled against God's wishes for them. Suffering is the result of their sin—their hatred of one another, their thoughtlessness toward the environment and the animal world. Not all suffering, however, is due to human sin.

Christians have debated this question down the centuries. In a sense, suffering is a mystery. When Job questioned God about the existence of suffering, God asked him: "Why do you talk without knowing what you are talking about?" (Job 38:2, *The Message*).

Another way is to explore the nature of God, to ask: "Would it help if God intervened every time someone was suffering?" In his book *Why Do People Suffer?* James Jones, a Church of England bishop, recalls an incident from his own life. As you read it, imagine that the father is God and the child is each of us in our suffering.

I remember once walking past the school at the end of our road. On the other side of the six-foot wall I could hear a small child crying inconsolably. A teacher was trying to comfort her but with little immediate success. Like any parent, the sound of a child sobbing stirred my heart.

As I walked on down the road, the child's crying ringing in my ears, I stopped dead in my tracks as I realized that the child who was in tears was my own daughter. Part of me wanted to vault over the wall and rescue her—to tell her that it was all right, that Daddy was here and she'd be okay now. But another part of me knew that I should do nothing of the *kind—that I had to leave her so that others could come near to her and help her.*[3]

In the end, there is no answer to the problem of suffering that will fully satisfy our reason. Perhaps the most important thing to say is that as Christians, we do not believe that God wills our suffering. He does not sit on a throne far away, deciding which of us will suffer today. On the contrary, the cross of Jesus means that God shares our suffering. God suffers alongside us. (See Chapter 4, "Jesus: death and resurrection.")

The cross, flowers, and stained glass are common symbols found in churches. How does each one speak to you about the nature of God? What other symbols of God are important to you?

Thinking it through

- Think about how you came to believe in God. What evidence is there of God's presence in the world?

- What do you understand prayer to be? Do you think that God answers prayers?

- How might James Jones's account of the father and his child help you to believe in a loving God in the face of suffering?

Bible Study

Read the following descriptions of God in the Bible:

Deuteronomy 32:6, 10
Isaiah 49:14-15
Psalm 18:2
1 Timothy 6:15
1 Corinthians 4:5

- Is God described in terms of gender (i.e. male or female)? What does this say about God?

- What do these descriptions say about God's relationship to people?

FOR PRAYER & REFLECTION

God be in my head
and in my understanding.
God be in my eyes
and in my looking.
God be in my mouth
and in my speaking.
God be in my heart
and in my thinking.
God be at mine end
and at my departing.

Some prayer **topics**

A prayer of thanks for all the good things God has created.

To say sorry for all the times when you have turned away from God and God's will for your life.

To ask God to come into the situation you find yourself in at the moment—to ask for God's help, protection and guidance.

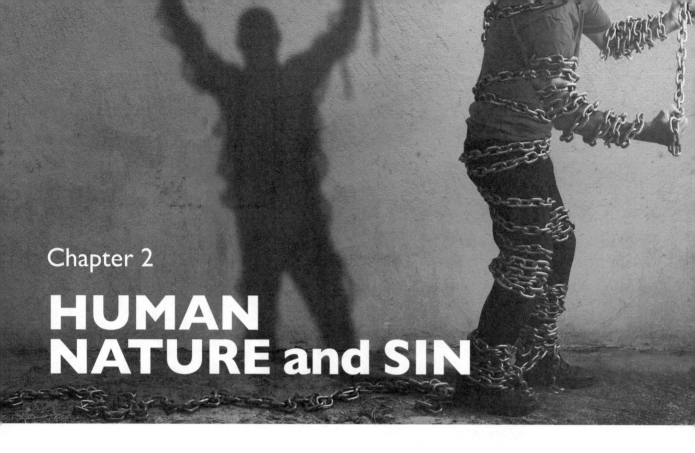

Chapter 2

HUMAN NATURE and SIN

A beautiful world often spoiled

The era from the beginning of the twentieth century to the present day has witnessed the best and worst of human nature—humanity displayed in its extreme forms. Human beings have put people on the moon and have achieved a medical revolution that includes heart transplants and antibiotics that can banish bacterial infections. Smallpox has disappeared from the planet, and many other infectious diseases are treatable. We can travel from the east coast of the United States to England in seven hours or Australia in a day and instant communication has created the impression, if not the reality, of a "global village."

However, the twentieth century saw millions of lives lost in countless wars—the First and Second World Wars, conflicts in Vietnam, Cambodia, and Yugoslavia, as well as Stalin's purges in Russia and the cultural revolution in China. Nor do the first two decades of the twenty-first century, in which wars and terrorist attacks have continued to cause extensive loss of life, mutilation, and human suffering, look much better.

Despite economic ups and downs, human beings now enjoy greater prosperity and stability in the world's rich countries than ever before, but wars and starvation still expose countless millions to unprecedented suffering.

The good aspects of life give us hope but the extent of evil in the world disturbs us. Evil threatens our happiness and security. People can be innocently traveling to work, attending school, and enjoying a concert, only to be horrifically attacked by gunfire or bombs.

Experiences like this can make us feel that human beings have missed the mark, that we have fallen far short of what we could be. We are like a marksman or archer aiming for a bull's-eye and missing the target.

Christians call this sense of falling short sin. Individual actions that make us fall short are sins.

What is sin?

At the heart of sin lies "I." Sin is **selfish**.

We sin when we turn away from God and worship someone or something else—for example, when we become obsessed with ourselves and our own happiness, or with wealth or status.

Russian author Fyodor Dostoevsky, in the following story from *The Brothers Karamazov*, illustrates this by describing a woman who is wicked (sinful) because she only thinks of herself.

Throughout history, evil has forced innocent people to seek safety elsewhere. This photograph shows refugees from Syria and Iraq fleeing the conflicts in their countries. Why do people do this to one another?

The wicked woman and the onion

There was once a very wicked woman who died and went to hell. Her guardian angel took pity on her and asked God whether there was anything that could be done to rescue her. God told the angel that he should search the record of her life for any good deed which she might have done. If he could find one, this could be used to save her. The angel went away and searched through the Book of Life and could not find anything to begin with. Eventually, though, he found one kind act. One day, a beggar had come to the woman asking for food. She had gone into her garden and pulled up an onion which she had given to the beggar. The angel returned to God and told him this. God then told the angel to go to the lake of fire and lift the woman out with the help of the onion. The angel went to the lake and called, 'Woman, woman.' She came swimming across the lake of fire and,

clasping on to the onion, was lifted from the fire. As this happened, others saw what was happening and they too were lifted from the lake by holding on to her feet and long skirt. For a moment, the wicked woman and several other people were being lifted from the lake. But then she felt the tugging of the other people on her feet and on her skirt. Looking down on them, she kicked them away from her. At that moment, the onion leaves which were supporting her snapped and she and all the others fell back into the lake of fire, where they are to this day. The angel went away and wept.[1]

In a word, the woman's selfishness spoils everything. Her selfishness means that not only she but also many others lose the chance of rescue.

Sin is like a poison, as this next story shows:

A man went to see his doctor because he had three nasty boils. He asked the doctor

Abuse of the environment—as well as of human communities—is an aspect of sin. What can you do to help heal the environment?

Christian beliefs about human nature and sin

• **Sin began with Adam and Eve in the Garden of Eden.** Although many do not take it as literal history, the story of Adam and Eve expresses deep Christian truths about human nature and sin. It is a description of how we are now, not of how we came to be this way. According to the story, Adam and Eve were placed in the Garden of Eden after they were created and had everything they needed. There was no shortage of food and they were in complete harmony with all the other creatures. They were without self-consciousness, and so they walked about the garden naked but without embarrassment, like very young children running naked around a sandy beach on a warm day. But they were given one command: they were forbidden to eat of the Tree of the Knowledge of Good and Evil. However, the serpent told Eve to ignore this command. Eve gave in to temptation and took fruit from this tree and tempted Adam to share it with her. By this disobedience, they "fell" from the harmonious relationship which they had with God. So this story is called "The Fall," and their sin is called "original sin" because it goes back to the origins of humanity.

• **The Fall had dire consequences.** The Bible lists the worst consequences of the Fall. Adam and Eve were banished from the Garden of Eden to a life of labor, ending in death, and Eve was to suffer pain in childbirth. They lost harmony with the natural world, a loss symbolized by the fear and hatred that comes about between them and the serpent. Their son, Cain, committed the first murder by killing his brother, Abel. Death, suffering, crime, and war continue to trouble us today.

to remove each of them. The doctor replied that there was no point in just treating these surface symptoms. There was a poison that had spread all over the man's body. Only when this had been treated would the boils go . . .

The human race is sick and has "boils" that affect it—think of the suffering caused by war and the lack of food. We would love to "cut them out" but we will never succeed unless we recognize the "poison within us" that causes them.

Michael Ramsey
Introducing the Christian Faith[2]

Sin spreads like a disease. Think of the way bullying spreads in a school. Once one or two incidents of bullying have gone unstopped, others feel emboldened and copy the behavior; bullying becomes a way of life.

Christians believe that sin may affect all aspects of life. This is particularly apparent in developed, "rich" countries.

- Death and pain are not what human beings were ultimately created for. The story of Adam and Eve paints a clear picture of the way that human beings have a capacity for misusing their free will, which results in death and pain. But it also shows us that Adam and Eve started out in a world free from them.

- God originally made human beings and the whole creation as something good, something that God loved and approved of. Human beings are made in the image of God. This means that we were created good and are, by nature, closer to God than anything else in creation. On a lesser scale, we are creators, as is shown by the arts, sciences, and human society itself.

- Closeness between God and humans is spoiled by human disobedience—but God doesn't leave it there. God made promises (covenants) with Noah, Abraham, and Moses, to whom God also gave laws, assuring them of favor as long as they and their people obeyed God's will. Often they failed, so God sent prophets to remind them of their promises. Finally, God sent Jesus to achieve reconciliation between God and humans, the atonement (see Chapter 4: "Jesus: death and resurrection" for more about this). The fact that God keeps trying to restore relations between God and human beings shows how important they are to God and how much God wants them to make something of their lives.

- But we are unable to be good or save ourselves just because we want to. However hard we try, we cannot rid our own lives or society of death, suffering, crime, and war, or any of the other things that spoil our lives. God has had to take the initiative in helping us.

- We need someone to help us: We need a Savior. We may make progress in organizing society, through better health services, better food and housing, and better education, but we never quite succeed. The twentieth century, which saw the greatest ever improvement in the quality of life in the United States and other wealthy countries, saw the greatest scale of war, destruction, and starvation as well.

- Jesus in his life and death restored human nature. In the New Testament, we learn how Jesus lived and how he wants us to live. We also discover how he defeated death and evil by dying on the cross and being raised to new life by God. He opens up the possibility of a new kind of human life. Our old fallen nature can be restored to its full potential.

- We can share in what Jesus did. By our becoming Christians, death and suffering will have no final power over us. Jesus teaches that all who follow him will suffer and die, but that they will also be given new life.

- Jesus' work in restoring human beings to the fullness of life that God intended is not over yet. There is still enormous suffering and evil in the world, and individual Christians continue to sin even after we have turned to Christ. We need the help of Jesus and other Christians, which we experience in worship and prayer, to help bring about the full reign of Jesus on earth and in heaven, what Christians call the kingdom of God. This will not be completed until Christ returns. The whole process, as Saint Paul says, is like a woman in labor, where suffering and struggle have to come before the birth of a new life.

Our greed for earth's resources has contributed to global climate change, which has caused both floods and droughts, depriving others of their homes, livelihood, and even lives. Moreover, our waste of food makes it more expensive for those living in poorer countries, who will as a result be undernourished or starve.

Some would say that the wastefulness of rich countries like ours has no bearing on poverty in other parts of the world. It's not as if the loaves of bread we're throwing away could actually be shipped to other countries.

But...grain, like many other foods, is a globally traded product, with a limited supply. If rich countries are wasting lots of the grain they buy, it stands to reason that they are buying more of it than they would otherwise need to. That unnecessarily high demand reduces the overall supply, which pushes the price up, making grain less affordable for poor and undernourished people in other parts of the world.

William Skidelsky[3]

The whole world, therefore, needs saving. This is why the gospels show Jesus restoring the sick to health and calming the storm. These stories show the way in which God can reverse the sin and disorder of every aspect of the world: "your iniquities have been barriers between you and your God, and your sins have hidden his face from you so that he does not hear" (Isaiah 59:2).

Sin separates us from those whom we love and from God, as this true story shows:

In America, in the 1990s, two brothers convicted of murder both offered to donate a kidney to their mother before they were executed.

She had raised nine other children successfully but her two youngest, ages 29 and 28, had a long history of wrongdoing. They drank heavily, took drugs, and got into trouble with the police from an early age. The younger of the two was convicted of rape at the age of 16 and spent two years in a juvenile detention center and seven in prison.

The two brothers and their cousin lured a 64-year-old man from a bar with a promise of more drinks at another bar. Afterwards, the man was found beaten to death. All three were convicted of first-degree murder and sentenced to death.

Meanwhile, their mother's kidney disease had worsened, and she was receiving dialysis to clean her blood three times a week. This meant hours attached to a machine, persistent poor health and the prospect of living only a little time longer. Doctors said her best chance lay with a transplant if the right donor could be found.

On death row, the younger brother offered a kidney to give his mother the chance to live. So did the elder brother when she went to visit him later. Doctors tested both brothers to see whether their kidneys were suitable for transplant. Even though the younger brother had been the first to offer, his kidney wasn't compatible. Fortunately, his elder brother's was, and their mother soon had a successful transplant at a hospital in Philadelphia.

The younger brother was executed by lethal injection. The elder brother, years later, is still on death row waiting for the date of his execution to be set. The mother was happy with her recovery but broken-hearted about her sons.[4]

This story shows how sin *separates*. It separated the two sons from ever living a normal life again. However, the story also shows that the good part of human nature is never completely lost—even in people who have committed the worst sins. These young men were still able to make sacrifices for someone they loved.

Thinking it through

- Are some sins worse than others?
- Does it help to see sin as a sickness? If sin is sickness, what is health?
- Discuss how this sickness affects:
  (a) the world;
  (b) your neighbourhood;
  (c) yourself.
- Why do you think some people do wrong from an early age?
- Do you think that anyone is "all bad?"
- How good are most people? Are some people wholly good—do you know anyone who is?

Bible Study

Read chapter 8 of Paul's letter to the Romans. In it, Paul sets out the hope we have in Jesus, that God's love will save the whole of Creation.
Reflect on these parts:

- How can the Holy Spirit help us? (verses 5-9, 26-27)
- How close can we be to God?
- How should we feel about suffering? (verses 13-18)
- How does this describe sin as affecting the whole creation? What hope does it hold out to us? (verses 19-25)

FOR PRAYER & REFLECTION

Prayers asking for protection from sin and danger:

Be our light in the darkness, O Lord,
*   and in your great mercy*
defend us from all perils and dangers
*   of this night; for the love of your*
only Son, our Savior Jesus Christ. Amen.

Visit this place, O Lord, and drive far
*   from it all snares of the enemy;*
let your holy angels dwell with us to
*   preserve us in peace;*
and let your blessing be upon us always;
through Jesus Christ our Lord. Amen.[5]

Some prayer **topics**

For help with overcoming selfishness.

That the world can be delivered from the sin that spoils it, especially war and the destruction of the environment.

For the strength to say 'no' to the sin which spreads through our lives.

That we should not be separated from one another by sin.

Chapter 3

JESUS: LIFE and MINISTRY

Do you believe in Jesus Christ, the Son of God?
I believe in Jesus Christ, his only Son, our Lord.
—*The Book of Common Prayer*, p. 304

Today more people follow Jesus Christ than anyone else on earth. Jesus' influence can be seen in the images in this chapter. Throughout the centuries, artists and illustrators have depicted Jesus in ways that make sense to them. Today, in Brazil Jesus is depicted as a Brazilian, in Korea as a Korean, and among the Maoris in New Zealand as a Maori. All cultures throughout the centuries have been influenced by Jesus Christ. But who is Jesus?

Who is Jesus?

A human being like us

Jesus was a man who walked the dusty streets, was tempted, as all people are, and died as a criminal on a cross. But in his teaching, people recognized that he spoke with an authority unlike anyone else. In his miracles, they saw an extraordinary power at work in him. Jesus was not an ordinary man, but he was still fully a human being. He shows the true potential of our human nature when it is perfectly united with God.

The Son of God

During his life Jesus would often go away to a quiet place to be alone with God. These times of quietness were one of the sources of his inner strength. Jesus spoke of the special relationship he had with God, whom he called "Father." According to John's Gospel, he identified himself with God the Father, telling his disciples that "The Father and I are one" (John 10:30) and that "If you knew me, you would know my Father also" (John 8:19).

As the early disciples thought about the life of Jesus, they came to believe that he was more than a human being. He was God's Son who came and lived as a man on earth. Matthew gave Jesus the name *Emmanuel*, which means "God is with us." The early Church came to refer to this belief as the *Incarnation*. The word means "in the flesh," and refers to the belief that God became a human being in Jesus.

John's Gospel begins with a poem describing the Incarnation (John 1:1-5, 14-18). In describing Jesus as the *Word* of God, Saint John is telling us that he is God's ultimate *self-expression* in human terms:

In the beginning was the Word, and the Word was with God, and the Word was God. He was in the beginning with God. All things came into being through him, and without him not one thing came into being. What has come into being in him was life, and the life was the light of all people. The light shines in the darkness, and the darkness did not overcome it . . .

This image shows a fresco of a black Madonna and Jesus in Axum Cathedral, Ethiopia. Why do you think artists from different countries often depict Jesus as a member of their community?

And the Word became flesh and lived among us, and we have seen his glory, the glory as of a father's only son, full of grace and truth. (John testified to him and cried out, "This was he of whom I said, 'He who comes after me ranks ahead of me because he was before me.'") From his fullness we have all received, grace upon grace. The law indeed was given through Moses; grace and truth came through Jesus Christ. No one has ever seen God. It is God the only Son who is close to the Father's heart, who has made him known.

17

Christian beliefs about Jesus

- **Jesus was a historical person who lived in the first century** . In addition to the four gospel accounts of his life (written between 30 and 60 years after Jesus' crucifixion), both Jewish (Josephus) and Roman historians (Tacitus, Pliny, and Suetonius) record his existence.

- **Jesus was Jewish.** His parents were Jewish, and he was circumcised on the eighth day in accordance with Jewish law (Luke 2:21).

- **Jesus was sent by God to save and rescue people.** The word "Jesus" (Hebrew "Joshua") means "God saves" or "God rescues." The gospel writers show that Jesus was special in a number of ways. They tell us his birth was heralded by angels: "The angel said to her, 'Do not be afraid, Mary, for you have found favor with God. And now, you will conceive in your womb and bear a son, and you will name him Jesus'" (Luke 1:30-31); God spoke to Joseph about the birth in dreams: "an angel of the Lord appeared to him in a dream and said, 'Joseph, son of David, do not be afraid to take Mary as your wife, for the child conceived in her is from the Holy Spirit'" (Matthew 1:20).

- **Jesus' birth was a virgin birth:** "Look, the virgin shall conceive and bear a son, and they shall name him Emmanuel" (Matthew 1:23).

- **Jesus was the Messiah whom the Jews had been eagerly awaiting.** At the time of Jesus, the Jews were eagerly waiting for God to send the Messiah who would rescue them from their Roman oppressors. Jesus' closest disciples, led by Peter, came to believe that Jesus was the Messiah: "He said to them, 'But who do you say that I am?' Peter answered, "The Messiah of God'" (Luke 9:20). Jesus intimated that he was the Christ: "Jesus said, 'I am; and 'you will see the Son of Man seated at the right hand of the Power', and 'coming with the clouds of heaven'" (Mark 14:62). But Jesus taught that he had not come to save the Jews from Roman rule but to save them from their sinful ways and to bring people back to God. He also taught that he had come not only for the Jews but for all people. Christians today call Jesus "Christ," which is the Greek word for Messiah.

- **Jesus came to bring in the kingdom of God.** Jesus summed up his message with the words: "The time is fulfilled, and the kingdom of God has come near; repent, and believe in the good news" (Mark 1:15). Jews understood the phrase "kingdom of God" to mean a state of accepting God as king of your life. In his teaching Jesus showed that the kingdom was already present in the lives of those people who had accepted God as ruler. But the kingdom was like a small mustard seed which had to grow into a large plant (Mark 4:30-32). God's kingdom was being established through Jesus' ministry of casting out evil spirits, healing ill people, raising people from the dead, and showing God's authority over nature.

- **Jesus was fully human.** One of Jesus' favorite titles for himself was the "Son of Man." This Hebrew expression means 'human being'. He saw himself as a Jewish man who was called to be obedient to God: "I do nothing on my own, but I speak these things as the Father has instructed me" (John 8:28).

- Jesus was fully divine. For Christians Jesus is more than a good man. They believe he is the Son of God. This belief is called incarnation—God "became flesh and lived among us, and we have seen his glory, the glory of a father's only son, full of grace and truth, lived among us" (John 1:14). At his baptism he heard a voice saying: "You are my own Son, the Beloved; with you I am well pleased" (Mark 1:11). Toward the end of Jesus' life, God spoke again through a cloud at Jesus' transfiguration: "This is my Son, the Beloved; listen to him!" (Mark 9:7). And Jesus often spoke of the special relationship he had with God. He called himself Son: "All things have been handed over to me by my Father; and no one knows the Son except the Father, and no one knows the Father except the Son and anyone to whom the Son chooses to reveal him" (Matthew 11:27). Christians believe that Jesus is the second person of the Trinity (God the Father, Son and Holy Spirit).

- Jesus shows us what God is like. When God became a human being in Jesus, he showed God's amazing love for us by coming "down to our level," to help us and to save us. In the gospels, Jesus is shown as someone who really cares about those who are rejected by society. We are called to follow Jesus' example: "Let the same mind be in you that was in Christ Jesus" (Philippians 2:5).

- Jesus' death and resurrection were the key events in his life. Through his death, it has been possible for us to be at one with God again. Jesus' resurrection gives us hope that death is not the end, that good triumphs over evil, and that our destiny is to be with God for ever.

The coming of God's kingdom changes the world

Jesus summed up his message by proclaiming at the beginning of his ministry, "The time is fulfilled, and the kingdom of God has come near; repent, and believe in the good news" (Mark 1:15). By the term "kingdom of God" he did not mean a place but, instead, the reign of God. He called people to follow him and to accept God as king of their lives. Jesus asks the same of us today.

But what did the reign of God mean? What sort of kingdom was Jesus bringing in? He gave a clear description of it when he spoke in the synagogue at Nazareth after his baptism. He read the following passage from the book of Isaiah:

> *"The spirit of the Lord is upon me,*
> *because he has anointed me*
> *to bring good news to the poor.*
> *He has sent me to proclaim release*
> *to the captives*
> *and recovery of sight to the blind,*
> *to let the oppressed go free,*
> *to proclaim the year of the Lord's favor."*
>
> *And he rolled up the scroll, gave it back to the attendant, and sat down. The eyes of all in the synagogue were fixed on him. Then he began to say to them, "Today this scripture has been fulfilled in your hearing."'*
>
> Luke 4:18-21

Jesus made the startling announcement that this scripture was being fulfilled in their presence: Jesus himself was bringing in God's rule over people's lives and over all the earth. God's rule over the earth would be good news for the poor and the

This mosaic of Jesus comes from the Hagia Sophia in Istanbul. Does it show the human or the divine person of Jesus? How can you tell?

One solitary life

He was born in an obscure village, the child of a peasant woman.

He grew up in still another village, where he worked in a carpenter's shop until he was 30.

Then for three years he was an itinerant preacher.

He never wrote a book.

He never held an office.

He never had a family or owned a house.

He didn't go to college. He traveled no more than 200 miles from the place where he was born.

He did none of the things one usually associates with greatness.

He had no credentials but himself.

He was only 33 when public opinion turned against him.

His friends ran away.

He was turned over to his enemies and went through the mockery of a show trial.

He was nailed to a cross between two thieves.

While he was dying, his executioners gambled for his clothing, the only property he had on earth.

When he was dead, he was laid in a borrowed grave through the pity of a friend.

Nineteen centuries have come and gone, and today he is the central figure of the human race, the leader of mankind's progress.

All the armies that ever marched,
all the navies that ever sailed,
all the parliaments that ever sat,
all the kings that ever reigned,
put together, have not affected
the life of man on earth
as much as that
One Solitary Life.[1]

downtrodden. God would fight on the side of justice and peace. Jesus had come to bring God's love to all people, especially those despised by society.

In the gospels, Jesus is often seen mixing with the outcasts of society (lepers, prostitutes, the poor). He came to show God's love for them.

Christians today continue to be called to follow Jesus in bringing about justice in the world. Many work alongside charities (both local and international) that seek to help people who are often ignored by the rest of society.

Jesus the teacher

When Jesus taught about the kingdom of God, he spoke with an authority that amazed people. His words had a power all of their own. He spoke of a God of love who taught that the greatest command was to love God with all your heart, soul, mind, and strength and to love your neighbor as you love yourself: "Jesus answered, 'The first is, 'Hear, O Israel: the Lord our God, the Lord is one; you shall love the Lord your God with all your heart, and with all your soul, and with all your mind, and with all your strength.' The second is this, 'You shall love your neighbor as yourself'' " (Mark 12:29-31). Jesus likened God to a father who accepts a wayward son back into his loving arms, to a shepherd who goes in search of the one lost sheep, and to a woman who searches diligently for a lost coin and rejoices when she finds it (Luke 15).

Jesus often taught in everyday stories called parables. His teaching has a power to change people's lives today, as the

priest and lecturer in economics Robert Van de Weyer experienced in his own life. One Christmas Day, Robert wrote in his diary:

I have decided to try an experiment: to make Jesus my teacher for a test period of six months. During this time I shall act as a full disciple, studying his teachings closely and following them as far as I can. Then on June 25 next year I shall stand back and review what has happened to me.[2]

During the next few months, Robert discovered that his unbelief in God started to give way. For example, just six weeks into his experiment, he wrote:

As I try to follow Jesus' instructions, my agnosticism is beginning to waver. When I am angry or depressed or in any other unloving mood, I make myself say little

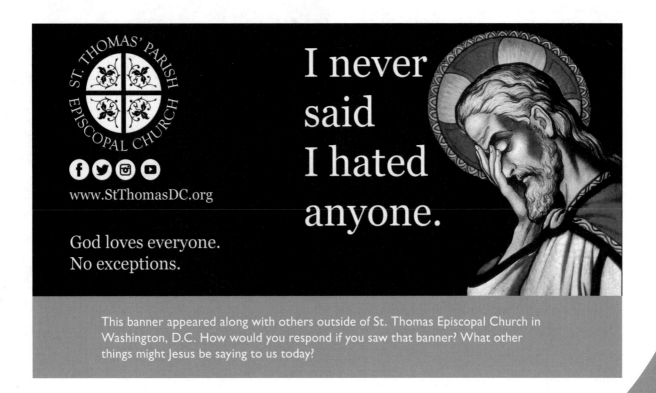

ST. THOMAS' PARISH EPISCOPAL CHURCH

www.StThomasDC.org

God loves everyone.
No exceptions.

I never said I hated anyone.

This banner appeared along with others outside of St. Thomas Episcopal Church in Washington, D.C. How would you respond if you saw that banner? What other things might Jesus be saying to us today?

prayers asking for help to overcome the mood. I do this because Jesus instructs me to. To my surprise I am generally finding the prayer works, and my bad mood quickly disappears . . . I also have the strong impression of an outside force working within me. It seems to demand my submission, and having submitted to it, I feel I have no control over it . . . I am also now aware of the force each evening as I say the Lord's Prayer when I reach the phrase "thy will be done." As I turn the phrase over in my mind I sense the presence of a will greater than my own, pressing upon me.[3]

Jesus the miracle worker

Jesus not only spoke about God's kingly rule, he also demonstrated it in his miracles. He showed God's loving compassion toward people who are sick, and God's power over sickness, evil, nature, and even death. Many people followed Jesus because of the miracles he performed by the power of God's Holy Spirit. After he had died and been raised from the dead and ascended to heaven, his apostles carried on his work. They also performed miracles, healing and restoring people to full health and rescuing them from all that oppressed them.

Christians believe that the power of Jesus to heal is still at work today. Some Christians, especially in the Charismatic or Pentecostal movement, still claim to experience miraculous healing, but often we experience the healing of spirit, soul, and body gradually, as we grow closer to God in prayer and the sacraments. (See Chapter 18 on the sacrament of anointing the sick.)

Jesus—a window into God

Jesus often spoke of the special relationship he had with God. He told his followers that "The Father and I are one." In John's Gospel Jesus uses seven sayings to describe himself. They all start with the words "I am."

This contemporary icon written by Mary Jane Miller is called "Christ Sees in the Trinity." How does this approach help you understand Jesus?

"I am the bread of life. Whoever comes to me will never be hungry, and whoever believes in me will never be thirsty" (John 6:35).

"I am the light of the world. Whoever follows me will never walk in darkness but will have the light of life" (John 8:12).

Jesus was no ordinary man. Jesus points the way to God, he is the Son of God, who gives meaning and purpose to our lives.

"I am the gate for the sheep . . . Whoever enters by me will be saved" (John 10:7, 9).

"I am the good shepherd. The good shepherd lays down his life for the sheep" (John 10:11).

"I am the resurrection and the life" (John 11:25).

"I am the way, and the truth, and the life. No one comes to the Father except through me" (John 14:6).

"I am the true vine, and my Father is the vine-grower" (John 15:1).

Joe Gibbs, a former head coach of the Washington Redskins football team, said:

A lot of people in the world would probably look at me and say: "Man, if I could just coach in the Super Bowl, I'd be happy and fulfilled..." But I'm here to tell you, it takes

"Jesus the Homeless" by Canadian sculptor Timothy Schmalz depicts Jesus as a homeless person, sleeping on a park bench. The sculpture has been installed in front of churches around the world. What message do you think the sculptor is trying to convey about Jesus and our relationship with him?

something else in your life besides money, position, football, power and fame. The vacuum in each of our lives can only be filled through a personal relationship with our Lord and Savior Jesus Christ. Otherwise, I'm telling you, we'll spend the rest of our lives in a meaningless existence. I've seen it in football players' eyes, and I've seen it in men who are on their death bed. There's nothing else that will fill that vacuum.

Quoted in Charles Colson,
The Body[4]

Jesus—God in the flesh (the Incarnation)

In the thirteenth century, Elizabeth was queen of Hungary. Although she was a wealthy woman. she did not forget those who had little. Many were poor because of a famine that had hit the land. She spent an enormous amount of her wealth on building hospitals, giving money to the poor, and providing homes for orphans. Tragedy struck Elizabeth's life when her husband died in a war. The courtiers in the palace took advantage of this to demand that Elizabeth justify giving away her royal money to the poor. They were themselves greedy and had no interest in the poor or in Elizabeth's Christian beliefs. Elizabeth was forced to make a decision between the poor and her royalty. She chose the poor and decided to sacrifice her wealth, her power, and even her family ties for them. She sacrificed the comfort and richness of her palace to live in the cold and damp conditions of the poor. She worked for them day and night: feeding, nursing, and loving them. Elizabeth died young, at 24. Her decision to live with the poor contributed to her death. However, her love of the poor is what she is remembered for.

This historical example is a word picture of what God did when he became human in the person of Jesus—it was a costly thing to do. Saint Paul expressed this in Philippians:

> *Let the same mind be in you that was in
>   Christ Jesus,*
> *who, though he was in the form of God,*
> *did not regard equality with God*
> *as something to be exploited,*
> *but emptied himself,*
> *taking the form of a slave,*
> *being born in human likeness.*
> *And being found in human form,*
> *he humbled himself*
> *and became obedient to the point of death—*
> *even death on a cross.*
>
> Philippians 2:5-8

What difference does it make that God became a man in Jesus? It makes a great difference to our understanding of God—now God is near.

David Edwards[6]

Thinking it through

- Discuss what you think Jesus meant by each of his "I am" sayings.

- What do you think of the following argument?

  I am trying here to prevent anyone saying the really foolish thing that people often say about Him: "I'm ready to accept Jesus as a great moral teacher, but I don't accept His claim to be God." That is the one thing we must not say. A man who was merely a man and said the sort of things Jesus said would not be a great moral teacher. He would either be a lunatic—on a level with the man who says he is a poached egg—or else he would be the Devil of Hell. You must make your choice. Either this man was, and is, the Son of God: or else a madman or something worse.

  C. S. Lewis, *Mere Christianity*[7]

Bible Study

Read the account of Jesus' meeting with the man who was blind from birth (John 9).

As you read this passage you will find that people's reactions to Jesus change throughout the story. This account compares two forms of blindness—physical blindness and spiritual blindness.

- How did Jesus heal the blind man? (verses 6-7)
- How does the blind man's description of Jesus change throughout the story? (verses 11, 17, 33, and 38)
- How does the Pharisees's description of Jesus change as the story progresses? (verses 16, 24)

FOR PRAYER & REFLECTION

Almighty God,
you have given us your
    only-begotten Son
to take our nature upon him
and to be born of a pure virgin:
Grant that we, who have been born again
and made your children by adoption
    and grace,
may daily be renewed
    by your Holy Spirit;
through our Lord Jesus Christ,
to whom with you
    and the same spirit
be honor and glory,
    now and for ever.
    Amen.[8]

Some prayer **topics**

That more people may hear the good news about Jesus.

For Jesus' spirit to live within us.

For courage to show the evidence of Jesus' teaching in our own lives.

Chapter 4

JESUS: DEATH and RESURRECTION

Whether it's President John F. Kennedy or the musician Prince, we are interested in the way people die. Some deaths have a power of their own. Some people even become famous because of the way they die. Sometimes, in the case with heroes and heroines: their deaths sum up their lives. This is certainly true in the case of Jesus. The gospel writers present Jesus' death as the climax of his life. They devote more pages of their books to his death than to any other part of his life. In Saint John's Gospel, Jesus himself points to his death as the fulfilment of his life. One of the last things he says from the cross is "It is finished." But why was his death so important?

Importance of Jesus' death

Artists throughout the centuries have taken the death and resurrection of Jesus as their subject. They have done so because they believed that these events continued to have significance and were not simply something that happened in the past to the historical Jesus.

The image at the start of this chapter is a painting from an altarpiece by Matthias Grünewald, painted between 1513 and 1515 for the chapel at the hospital for plague victims in the small village of Isenheim. Imagine the patients ill with the plague, with no modern drugs or painkillers and little chance of recovery. They would have wondered what was the point of their lives. They would have asked the questions which all people ask when confronted by suffering and death: "How can God help?" and "What does he know of human suffering like ours?"

The picture suggests two answers:

- On the altar they saw Christ, their God, with the same festering ulcers as their own. It would have helped them to believe that they were not left on their own. Jesus is the God-who-suffers-with-us.

- The altar panels on which the crucified Lord is depicted open up to show a picture of the resurrection. To the question "How can God help?" comes the answer: the body that hung there dead on the cross is transformed into the body that gives off a dazzling light. This is what we can hope for and look forward to: we too will be given a "resurrection body."

Why did Jesus have to die?

Christians believe that through his death Jesus mended the broken relationship between God and humanity that had been caused by sin. He made us "at one" again with God, enabling God and humanity to freely communicate with each other. This is known as the atonement (at-one-ment).

A picture that can be seen at the British military camp, Catterick, helps us understand this. Painted during World War I, it shows a signaller lying dead in no-man's-land. He had been sent out to repair a cable broken down by shellfire. There he lies, cold in death, but with his task accomplished; for beside him lies the rejoined section of cable. Beneath the picture stands one word: "THROUGH."

On the cross Jesus put himself in our place and knew humanity's separation from God. This made him cry out the terrifying words, "My God, why have you forsaken me?" Although he was the Son of God, on the cross Jesus shared the pain and terror of our lostness. He came to be where we are, in order to bring us

This painting is part of the same altarpiece as the crucifixion scene on page 26. What ideas about Jesus' resurrection are expressed by this painting? Why do you think the artist thought it was important to portray both Jesus' crucifixion and resurrection?

back into his own relationship of union with the Father.

Christians have a number of different ways of understanding how Jesus did this, how he atoned for us. It is as if what happened on the cross was so vast that no one view can take it all in. Some see Jesus' offering of his life on the cross as the supreme example of God's love. Others believe Jesus died instead of us or he offered himself as a sacrifice.

The example of God's love

Jesus' death on the cross shows us just how much God loves and cares for us. But we can find this hard to grasp, as Saint Paul wrote: "I pray that you may have the power to comprehend...what is the breadth and length and height and depth, and to know the love of Christ that surpasses knowledge" (Ephesians 3:18-19).

We might take a cue from the images of Saint Paul's language and try to visualize the extent of God's love:

- **How long is it?** God's love endures throughout our earthly lives and into eternity;

- **How deep is it?** God's love can reach us wherever we are, whatever happens to us—no amount of despair or mess in our lives is beyond God's reach;

- **How high is it?** God's love can draw us into the closest relationship with him.

Then, when we contemplate the scale of God's love, we may be moved to believe that if God can do this—die on the cross—for us, we should be moved to change and no longer live selfish lives separated from God. We will be moved to repentance and become better people—the example of God's love will have saved us.

In Jesus God takes our place on the cross

Maria Skobtsova was a Russian nun who lived in a convent in Paris during World War II. When the Germans occupied the city, she felt God was calling her to the risky mission of feeding and hiding Jews. She realized this could easily lead to her imprisonment and death, but she believed that "each of us is called to follow Christ and give himself for his friends." All went well for a month. She hid hundreds of Jews in the convent and helped many escape France. However, at the end of the month the Gestapo came. Mother Maria was sent to Ravensbrück concentration camp.

At the camp the German guards came to refer to her as "that wonderful Russian nun." Many sensed the presence of God in her. She spent two and a half years in the camp. Then one day a group of women were lined up outside a building with a sign that said "baths" (but was in fact a gas chamber for killing people). One woman became hysterical. Calmly, Mother Maria took her place in the line and became her substitute. She passed through the doors and into the gas chambers. It was Good Friday, 1945.

Maria Skobtsova died in the place of the scared woman about to be killed. Christians believe that, in Jesus, God died in our place because he loves us.

Jesus defeated Satan

Placing Jesus on the cross made it appear that evil had defeated good. However, the resurrection demonstrates Christ's victory over evil—Jesus went through death to new resurrected life. Satan and the powers of darkness could not hold Jesus in the grave.

Jesus died as a sacrifice for us

We can use the word "sacrifice" to explain Jesus' death. Jesus did not resist his death —he went as a willing sacrifice, similar to how soldiers sacrifice their lives in order to make victory possible. Jesus wanted to show us how much he loved us—it was a costly sacrifice. The Bible describes it by saying: "For God so loved the world that he gave his only Son, so that everyone who believes in him may not perish but may have eternal life" (John 3:16).

An example of what it means to be a sacrifice is found in the life of Óscar Romero, archbishop of San Salvador in the late 1970s. During this period, numerous South American countries abandoned human rights in the pursuit of economic success. Many Christians spoke out against the many injustices. Between 1968 and 1979, approximately 1,500 priests, nuns and active lay people were arrested, kidnapped, interrogated, tortured, defamed, exiled, or assassinated. Romero was part of this protest and pledged "to let my blood be a seed of freedom and the sign that hope will soon be a reality." He was assassinated while saying Mass on March 24, 1980.

Romero was willing to sacrifice his life in order to show God's love for the poor. Since 1980 the Church in El Salvador has grown in strength and numbers. In the same way Jesus wanted to show us how much he loved us—it was a costly sacrifice.

Jesus died as a ransom

Our lives often seem to be held hostage by the devil—we have an inclination to do what is wrong. Kidnappers demand ransoms to free hostages. We believe that **Jesus was our ransom**—he paid the price to buy our freedom: "For the Son of Man came not to be served but to serve, and

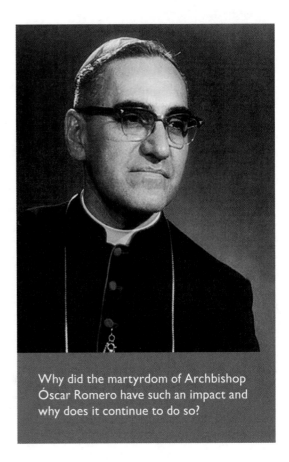

Why did the martyrdom of Archbishop Óscar Romero have such an impact and why does it continue to do so?

to give his life a ransom for many" (Mark 10:45).

Jesus rose from the dead

We believe that Jesus' death was not the end of the story. Jesus rose from the dead and was seen by many. Although there is no description of the actual event of the resurrection in the gospels, members of the early Church were convinced of it for three reasons:

1 The tomb was empty.

2 Jesus appeared to people after his death.

3 They felt his presence among them.

The resurrection is proof that good is greater than evil, life is stronger than death, and love is stronger than hate. The resurrection appearances show Jesus still with the marks of suffering on his body.

The festival of Easter celebrates both the death and resurrection of Jesus. Not only does it celebrate what Jesus did for us by dying for us but it also celebrates the fact that death is not the end. Jesus rose from the dead and by his resurrection gave us hope that we shall also be resurrected from the dead. We use light as a symbol of this new life.

We experience the results of the resurrection in our lives today. One of the earliest Christians to experience the risen presence of Jesus was Saint Paul. His conversion is recorded three times in the Acts of the Apostles (9:1-19; 22:6-16; 26:12-18). Christians all over the world feel Jesus' presence in their lives.

The resurrection means that Jesus is still living. He is living in our lives today and gives us hope for tomorrow.

Sam, 17

I see signs of resurrection life in every successful struggle against evil. Think of the eventual success of the civil rights movement in the United States or the struggle against apartheid in South Africa.

Jill, 19

Jesus ascended into heaven

After forty days, the book of Acts says, Jesus returned (ascended) to heaven. This is the Bible's way of telling us that although Jesus is no longer bound by the limitations of ordinary existence, nevertheless he is still alive and present to those who believe in him in all places and at all times.

Christian beliefs about Jesus' death and resurrection

• Jesus died by being nailed to a cross. This was the usual method of execution for a criminal in the Roman Empire. Jesus was crucified at the age of 33 on the order of Pontius Pilate, the Roman governor, after a trial in the Jewish High Court. Jewish and Roman (Gentile) involvement in Jesus' death highlights the fact that Jesus died for all sinful humanity. No one group of people was responsible for his death.

• Through Jesus' death humankind and God were brought together again.

• What Jesus accomplished was good. Through his death, Jesus showed us how much God loves us—enough to send his Son to die for us.

Thinking it through

- We have given President Kennedy and Prince as examples of people whose deaths made a lasting impression on the public. Think of some others and explain why they are important to you. You might choose famous people or those known to you personally.

- Which of the approaches to the atonement (sacrifice, ransom, etc.) makes most sense to you? What are your reasons?

- How do Christians remind themselves of Jesus' death and resurrection when they worship?

Bible Study

Read the Gospel accounts of the crucifixion of Jesus (Matthew 27:45-56; Mark 15:33-41; Luke 23:44-49; John 19:28-30).

Although the gospels have much in common, some distinct differences exists between the accounts, so read carefully.

- What did Jesus say from the cross? Discuss what these sayings mean.

- What elements in these accounts suggest that something more than an ordinary death was taking place? (Take note of what happened to the sky, etc.)

- How did people react to watching Jesus' death?

FOR PRAYER & REFLECTION

Almighty God, who through your only-begotten Son Jesus Christ overcame death and opened to us the gate of everlasting life:
Grant that we, who celebrate with joy the day of the Lord's resurrection, may be raised from the death of sin by your life-giving Spirit;
through Jesus Christ our Lord, who lives and reigns with you and the Holy Spirit, one God, now and for ever. Amen.[1]

Some prayer **topics**

Thank God for the love God has shown us by sending his Son to die on the cross.

Ask for forgiveness of our sins—for ways in which we deny God's love for us.

Give praise that God in Jesus has won the victory over evil, giving us all new life.

Chapter 5

The HOLY SPIRIT

Do you believe in God the Holy Spirit?

I believe in the Holy Spirit.

—*The Book of Common Prayer*, p. 304

Christianity: a supernatural religion

Do you believe in the supernatural? Do you believe that there is a spiritual dimension that operates alongside physical reality? Do you believe God actually speaks to people today? Do you believe God performs miracles today? Do you believe people can completely change, for example from being a drug pusher to being a parish priest?

Christians answer "yes" to each of these questions. Christianity is not just a set of beliefs, or a moral code. It is a supernatural religion—it is based on the belief that there is a reality above (*super* in Latin) or alongside the natural world. God did not just create the world in the beginning like some divine watchmaker and then sit back and let it tick away. God is actively involved in it. God's supernatural power is alive and well today in the form of the Holy Spirit, and it is at work in people to change them.

The power to change

Sometimes it is very difficult, if not impossible, to change bad habits of our own free will. However, when a person becomes a Christian he or she begins a new life. With the help of the Holy Spirit a self-centered life starts to become a God-centered one. Old habits begin to change, sometimes quite dramatically, as the following story illustrates.

Corrie Ten Boom was a Dutch woman who suffered under the Nazis in a concentration camp during World War II, and her sister Betsy had died in a camp. One day after the war, an ex-guard came to a church where Corrie was preaching. He sought her forgiveness for all the murders he had committed.

I stood there—I whose sins had again and again to be forgiven by God—and I could not forgive. I stood there with the coldness clutching my heart, "Jesus help me!" I prayed silently. "I can lift my hand. You supply the feeling." And so I thrust my hand into the one stretched out to me. And as I did, an incredible thing took place. The current started in my shoulder, raced down my arm and this healing warmth seemed to flood my whole being. I had never known God's love so intensely as I did then.

Corrie Ten Boom, *Tramp for the Lord* [1]

Corrie was able to forgive even her sister's murderers because the power of God's Holy Spirit had given her the power to do so.

God's miraculous power

The Bible tells us that the apostles traveled from town to town healing people by the power of God's Holy Spirit.

This Russian icon of Pentecost shows the Mother of God sitting on an elevated throne, surrounded by the apostles, with the Holy Spirit appearing above. What do you think about this depiction?

Christian beliefs about the Holy Spirit

- The Holy Spirit is the third person of the Trinity. God reveals and is experienced as Father, Son and Holy Spirit. God the Father creates and sustains the world. God the Son came into the world and "dwelt among us" as a human being, who was both divine and human. God the Holy Spirit is God in action in our world.

- The Holy Spirit is God with us now. We can see this throughout the account the gospels give of Jesus' life: at his baptism, the Spirit appeared as a dove; the Spirit drove Jesus into the wilderness to be tempted by the devil; it was by the power and with the help of the Spirit that Jesus performed his miracles and taught—the people listening to Jesus recognized that he spoke as one with special authority and power. Jesus told his disciples that when he had gone from them, "the Holy Spirit, whom the Father will send in my name, will teach you everything, and remind you of all that I have said to you" (John 14:26). After his death and resurrection, all the believers were gathered together when the Holy Spirit came upon them in power (see Acts 2). The Church celebrates this event today at Pentecost (also called Whit Sunday).

- The Holy Spirit is the life-giving Spirit. The words used for Spirit in the Bible (Old Testament *ruach*; New Testament *pneuma*) can mean "breath" or "wind." In the Old Testament story of the creation of the world, God gave Adam the breath of life and he became a living being. Without breath, there would be no life. On the day of Pentecost, the coming of the Holy Spirit is depicted as rushing wind (and tongues of fire). Throughout the Bible the Holy Spirit is shown actively at work in people to give them new life, God's life.

- The Holy Spirit distributes among Christians a variety of spiritual gifts that help them to obey Jesus' command to carry on his work. No believer is without a gift. Different kinds of special gifts include service, healing, preaching, discernment and speaking in tongues (see 1 Corinthians 12:4-11). The Charismatic movement (see page 36) has made people more aware of these spiritual gifts. Also, the Church teaches about the sevenfold gifts of the Spirit, which can be traced to Isaiah 11:1-3:

> A shoot shall come out from the stock of Jesse,
> and a branch shall grow out of his roots.
> The spirit of the LORD shall rest on him,
> the spirit of wisdom and understanding,
> the spirit of counsel and might,
> the spirit of knowledge and the fear of the LORD.
> His delight shall be in the fear of the LORD.

The seven gifts are:

Wisdom—to see things as God sees them.

Understanding—of God's revelation to us.

Counsel—to help us to see what we should do in difficult situations.

Inward Strength—to do God's will.

Knowledge—of the truth.

True Godliness—to feel that we are in a loving relationship with God and that we are brothers and sisters to all people.

Fear of the Lord—to give us an earnestness to do what God wishes.

At confirmation the bishop prays a special prayer over the candidates, asking the Holy

Spirit to supply them with all seven of these gifts to help them in their Christian life.

• **The Holy Spirit works in the lives of believers in a number of ways:**

– The Spirit lives in believers, making a home in their hearts: Saint Paul in his letter to the Christians at Ephesus hopes that they will "be strengthened in [their] inner being with power through his Spirit, and that Christ may dwell in [their] hearts through faith" (Ephesians 3:16-17).

– The Spirit gives life to them: As Saint Paul writes to the Christians in Rome, "If the Spirit of him who raised Jesus from the dead dwells in you, he who raised Christ from the dead will give life to your mortal bodies" (Romans 8:11).

– The Spirit helps people to pray: "the Spirit helps us in our weakness; for we do not know how to pray as we ought, but that very Spirit intercedes with sighs too deep for words" (Romans 8:26).

– The Spirit helps believers to become more like Jesus. The Holy Spirit gives people power to live as Christians. It works in people, transforming their characters so that they become more like Jesus. The qualities the Spirit develops in people are known as the fruit of the Holy Spirit: "the fruit of the Spirit is love, joy, peace, patience, kindness, generosity, faithfulness, gentleness, and self-control" (Galatians 5:22-23). This process of changing into the likeness of Jesus is called "sanctification" (being made holy). Saint Paul summarizes the gradual process of sanctification in this way: "[We]... are being transformed into the same image from one degree of glory to another; for this comes from the Lord, the Spirit" (2 Corinthians 3:18).

• **The Holy Spirit helps people to understand what God has revealed in the Bible.** Christians ask God to speak to them through the scriptures. It is the Holy Spirit who helps them to grasp the meaning of God's words. Without the Holy Spirit, the biblical account can seem dull and meaningless, but it can open our hearts and ears to hear God speaking to us through the words of the Bible.

• **To be filled with the Holy Spirit is never a once-and-for-all experience.** Christians are to ask continually for God to give them the Holy Spirit. Sometimes the Holy Spirit will come in memorable ways, as it did on the day of Pentecost. But sometimes the Holy Spirit works in quieter ways—to make our faith stronger, to give us courage, to guide us, etc.

• **The Holy Spirit is the power of God at work in the sacraments, for example:**

– at baptism: The making of new Christians is the work of the Holy Spirit in us. As Jesus put it: "no one can enter the kingdom of God without being born [again] of water and Spirit" (John 3:5). Jesus talked about the Holy Spirit as "living water" (John 7:37-39). Water is a symbol of life as well as a cleansing agent. Both these images are important ways of speaking about what the Holy Spirit does at baptism.

– at the center of the eucharist. Here there is a prayer to the Holy Spirit: "Grant that by the power of the Holy Spirit, these gifts of bread and wine may be to us his body and blood." God's power is at work in the form of the Holy Spirit to make Jesus present in the bread and wine, and present in our lives.

Fire is a common symbol for the Holy Spirit. It burns things away and can create space for new growth. Fire can represent the strength and power of the Holy Spirit to transform lives.

be healed so that a better quality of life is obtained." She illustrates this in her novel *A Question of Integrity*, based on real life experience:

> *Alice is interested in the people who go up to the altar for the laying on of hands and she's particularly interested in a stroke victim in a wheelchair. Alice sees that the stroke victim is not cured but in some mysterious way she's much healed because when the wheelchair comes back down the aisle after the laying on of hands the victim's face is radiant—her mood is quite changed.*[2]

Some people think that such events do not happen today. However, there are instances of healing that cannot be accounted for by conventional medicine. Also, there are many occasions when, although they may not recover physically, sick people have had their sense of inner, mental wholeness restored by prayer.

Susan Howatch explains this well: "Christian healers make a distinction between a cure and a healing. Not everyone can be cured of whatever physical and mental illness afflicts them, but spiritual and emotional wounds can

The Charismatic movement

We say that someone has "charisma" or is "charismatic" as a way of indicating that that person has a compelling charm. Christians use the term charismatic when talking about the gifts of the Holy Spirit, including signs, miracles, speaking in tongues, interpretation of tongues, healing, and discernment of spirits and prophecy. Before the twentieth century, people who received these gifts tended to leave their church and found a new group. In the twentieth century, though, many stayed within their churches, becoming known collectively as the Charismatic movement. Charismatics tend to see the gifts of the Spirit as an opportunity for renewal and revitalization within the Church.

Thinking it through

Saint Paul talks about the fruits of the Spirit (Galatians 5:22-23)—they are the qualities of character which the Holy Spirit creates in a person. Try to recall any occasion when you have been feeling bad about somebody and have asked God to give you the power to love that person. What happened?

- In what ways have you felt God's Holy Spirit working in your life?

- Have you experienced anything you would consider miraculous—the result of God's supernatural power at work?

- Have you heard of the Charismatic movement in the Church? If not, ask your priest to explain it.

Bible Study

Before his death, Jesus told his disciples that it would be necessary for him to go away in order that the Holy Spirit might come to be their helper (John 15:26; 16:7). On the fiftieth day after Easter, at Pentecost, Jesus' followers were all gathered in Jerusalem. Suddenly the power of the Holy Spirit came upon them. Read the account in Acts 2:1-4.

- What did the multitude see and hear? Although you cannot see wind, you can see the results of its power. Similarly you can see the power of the Holy Spirit in people's lives, changing them. Like fire, the Holy Spirit burns away things that are wrong, clearing the way for new growth. Fire is a symbol of God's presence.

- In what ways were the apostles changed people when they received the power of the Holy Spirit in their lives? Think about how they had reacted when Jesus was arrested and crucified and how they started to spread the gospel after the giving of the Holy Spirit.

FOR PRAYER & REFLECTION

O God, who on this day taught the hearts
*   of your faithful people*
*   by sending to them the light of your*
*   Holy Spirit:*
Grant us by the same Spirit to have a
*   right judgment in all things,*
*   and evermore to rejoice in his holy*
*   comfort;*
through Jesus Christ your Son our Lord,
*   who lives and reigns with you,*
in the unity of the Holy Spirit, one God,
*   for ever and ever. Amen.* [3]

Some prayer **topics**

Ask the Holy Spirit to enter into your life to:

- help you to become more like Jesus;

- change habits and attitudes;

- help you understand the Bible.

Chapter 6

The CHURCH

A worldwide community

The Church in the widest sense is the community of all the baptized, both the living and the departed, who are all related to Christ and to each other through their baptism. This, the Universal Church, is a spiritual reality that transcends membership of individual denominations (the Episcopal Church, the Roman Catholic Church, the Methodist Church, etc.). We also use the word to describe the place where God's people gather together for worship.
—*The Book of Common Prayer*, p. 304

In the United States, every city and virtually every town has a church. The same goes for villages, towns, and cities in Europe, South America, Africa, and many other parts of the world. Often these churches are the oldest buildings in their community.

For generations, the followers of Jesus have needed somewhere to meet and worship. This remains the same today. While some people may go to church infrequently, we still need large spaces in which to gather for Sunday worship, weddings, funerals, baptisms, and festivals—particularly Christmas and Easter.

Wherever the Church has met its members have needed a special building, a church. But the Church is first and foremost not a building. It is we ourselves, the people who belong to Christ.

The Body of Christ

Jesus taught that he came to save sinners: his intention was not to invite just a select few but everyone who responded to his call. The result of this was that the Christian Church from its very beginning has welcomed people regardless of their religious, ethnic, or social status. In this way, the Church follows Jesus' example of accepting those whom the rest of society has rejected. The most famous declaration of the openness of the Church can be found in Saint Paul's letter to the Christians in Galatia:

> *As many of you as were baptized into Christ have clothed yourselves with Christ. There is no longer Jew or Greek, there is no longer slave or free, there is no longer male and female; for all of you are one in Christ Jesus.*
> Galatians 3:27-28

Saint Paul believed that through baptism, a Christian became part of "the Body of Christ." As limbs and organs each have their part in the body, so do individual Christians within the life of the Church. Paul writes: "For just as the body is one and has many members, and all the members of the body, though many, are one body, so it is with Christ" (1 Corinthians 12:12).

The People of God

"The People of God" is another name for the Church. The first letter of Peter to the churches of Asia Minor describes them as "a chosen race, a royal priesthood, a holy nation, God's own people, in order that you may proclaim the mighty acts of him who called you out of darkness into his marvellous light" (1 Peter 2:9).

Membership of this people is open to all who respond to God's call to discipleship. This includes the poor and outcast. This means that the Church today has to be open to everyone and avoid showing racial or social prejudice.

One Church

Anglicans proclaim that they are part of one, holy, catholic and apostolic Church.

One: Although the "visible" Church (i.e. the Church as an institution) is divided, all Christians believe in one God and the one Lord Jesus Christ; and many churches and denominations recognize one another's baptism. In Christ we are all members of the one Christian Church, even though it is divided into different "structures" in the world.

Holy: We tend to use this word to mean especially good, but its Old Testament meaning includes a sense of someone or something being set aside or dedicated to God. To call the Church "holy" means that it is dedicated to God.

We shouldn't, therefore, expect the Church to be a community of people

The Church includes all people, young and old, of all races and ethnicities, socio-economic backgrounds, and political persuasions. In 2018, youth from across the Episcopal Church participated in General Convention, the primary legislative body. What roles do you think youth should play in the local congregation and the wider Church?

who are unfailingly good but a community of people trying to be good, dependent upon God's help and forgiveness. The first letter of John reminds us of this: "If we say that we have no sin, we deceive ourselves, and the truth is not in us. If we confess our sins, he who is faithful and just will forgive us our sins and cleanse us from all unrighteousness" (1 John 1:8-9).

If we dedicate ourselves to God, God will help us to change.

Catholic: This is a word with many different meanings. People often use it to mean Roman Catholic. But its underlying meaning is "universal."

Christians believe that Christ is present in a full or "whole" way wherever people pray or are gathered to worship him.

Catholic can also have the additional meaning of "possessing the whole faith." Anglicans believe that they have faithfully received and handed on the faith of the apostles.

Apostolic: This reminds us that our faith derives ultimately from the apostles and has been handed down faithfully since

The origins and growth of the Church

- **Origins:** The Christian Church has its origins in the group of disciples whom Jesus gathered at the beginning of his ministry. They deserted him at his arrest and crucifixion but regrouped to be the first witnesses of his resurrection and to continue his work once he had ascended into heaven. They formed the first Church (in Greek *ecclesía*, meaning "those called together") in Jerusalem. They were equipped for their work by the gift of the Spirit at Pentecost.

- **The early Church:** The members of this early Church lived a very simple life and continued to preach the gospel and heal people as Jesus had done. Through the work of Saint Peter and Saint Paul in particular, offshoots of this Church were planted all over the Roman Empire. As early Christian communities all over the known world took root, they kept in touch with one another and believed that the Holy Spirit bound them together. As the apostles died, they handed authority to bishops, to continue their leadership in the churches they had founded.

- **Leadership and unity:** The bishops were an important sign of this unity. They were a focus for the churches in their oversight (which formed a "see", i.e. "something overseen" or in the Episcopal Church, a diocese) and were also linked to one another. This link was expressed by their common defense of the truth of the Christian faith. By handing on authority through the ordination of bishops in every generation, a link was also maintained with the original apostolic faith. Bishops were assisted by deacons, and by priests who ran parishes for them. This unity of Christians has been disrupted many times in the past 2,000 years, most notably in 1054, when East and West divided, and in the sixteenth century when the Reformation occurred.

- **The Anglican Church** began when the Church of England removed itself from the Pope's authority at the Reformation, but it kept the historic ministry of bishops, priests, and deacons in unbroken succession. British colonies had their that time. Belief in Christ is rooted in historical events and the trustworthy public transmission of witness to them.

Bishops, priests, and deacons

The service of baptism reminds us that all Christians belong to a "royal priesthood" called to serve Christ and our "neighbor". However, in the churches that have bishops (e.g. Roman Catholic, Orthodox and Anglican), some Christians are called to serve in the three "orders" of ministry—bishops, priests, and deacons—whose roots can be detected in 1 Timothy, Acts and elsewhere in the New Testament.

own offshoots of the Church of England, which eventually became independent Anglican provinces. This family of churches is known as the Anglican Communion and numbers about 80 million members worldwide. The Archbishop of Canterbury, as the senior bishop (or "first among equals") of the Anglican Communion, invites bishops from around the world to meet together every ten years. This meeting is known as the Lambeth Conference after Lambeth Palace, the archbishop's London home, where the first conference was held.

- When the United States was a new country, Anglicans set up an independent church with the spirit of the emerging nation. Within the Episcopal Church, lay people, deacons, priests, and bishops each play their roles in governing the church. The Episcopal Church is an international church, with congregations in at least sixteen nations.

- Lay people (those not ordained) play an increasing role in the life and work of the churches of the Anglican Communion today. The top authority in the Episcopal Church is the General Convention, a gathering every three years in which lay people and clergy make democratic decisions about the church. Beneath this structure are diocesese and church councils (vestries). It is important to remember that all Christians, not just clergy, have a vocation—a calling to some special ministry or service for Christ in his Church.

- The Church includes all people, young and old, of all races and ethnicities, socio-economic backgrounds, and political persuasions. In 2018, youth from across the Episcopal Church participated in General Convention, the primary legislative body. What roles do you think youth should play in the wider Church? Are youth valued and respected in your local church?

Bishops, priests, deacons, and lay leaders come together as the Church to protest gun violence. What issues do you think your local church should protest or take public action to address?

Thinking it through

- What is the Anglican Communion? How is the Episcopal Church connected to the Communion?

- How would you respond to someone who said, "I can be a Christian without going to church?"

Bible Study

Read Acts 2:41-47.

This passage gives us a description of life in the first Christian Church to be formed after Jesus' resurrection and ascension. Its simplicity of life has provided an ideal to countless generations of Christians since.

- What were the main features of life in the earliest Christian Church described in this passage?

- Does it differ from the Church as you know it?

- What changes should we seek in the life of the church to which we belong?

FOR PRAYER & REFLECTION

Almighty and everliving God...Receive these our prayers which we offer unto thy divine Majesty, beseeching thee to inspire continually the Universal Church with the spirit of truth, unity, and concord: and grant that all they that do confess thy holy Name may agree in the truth of thy holy Word, and live in unity, and godly love.[1]

Some prayer **topics**

For the life of the Christian community to which you belong.

For particular people both in our community and elsewhere who need our prayers.

For our bishop and other parishes in the diocese.

For the worldwide Church, especially those who find it difficult to meet and worship and who may be persecuted for their faith.

Chapter 7
The CREEDS

The Episcopal Church is part of the one holy catholic and apostolic Church and professes the faith uniquely revealed in Holy Scripture and set forth in the catholic creeds.

When you read a long report, it will often have a bullet point summary at the beginning. New machines usually come with an exhaustive user's guide but they may have a quick start-up guide as well. And books usually have a blurb to tell you what they are about.

The creeds of the Christian Church are a bit like this. They are phrased in more formal language but they provide a kind of "back cover" or "bullet point summary for the Christian faith. They give you an idea of what you're going to get when you read on and know more.

They are used in church at many services and provide a summary of what the faith is about.

The two most widely used creeds are the Apostles' Creed and the Nicene Creed.

The Apostles' Creed

I believe in God, the Father almighty,
creator of heaven and earth.
I believe in Jesus Christ, his only Son, our Lord,
who was conceived by the power of the
Holy Spirit, and born of the Virgin Mary.
He suffered under Pontius Pilate,
was crucified, died, and was buried.
He descended to the dead.
On the third day he rose again.
He ascended into heaven,
and is seated at the right hand of the Father.

This thirteenth-century illuminated manuscript illustrates the "twelve articles of faith set out by twelve apostles." The Apostles' Creed is probably the best-known form of the creed in the West; the Nicene Creed is also very familiar to Episcopalians as it is frequently said at the eucharist.

He will come again to judge the living and
*   the dead.*
I believe in the Holy Spirit,
the holy catholic Church,
the communion of saints,
the forgiveness of sins,
the resurrection of the body,
and the life everlasting.
*   Amen.*[1]

The creed begins by acknowledging God as the Creator of the world and spelling out Jesus' relationship to him: he is God's "only Son," "born of the Virgin Mary." He is unique. Then the great acts of his life are outlined: he suffered, died and was buried at a particular time in history (we know this from the reference to Pontius Pilate, whose life is independently

Facts about the creeds

A "creed" has come to be recognized as a concise, formal, and universally accepted and authorized statement of the main points of Christian faith.
    Alister McGrath, *Christian Theology*[2]

- **Creeds are summaries of Christian belief** that developed from the questions asked by bishops at baptism. However, it is important to realize that they also play the role of a standard or coat of arms. We are meant to rally to them.

- People rally round a flag to signify that they belong to a group. In the same way, Christians say the creeds together as a way of showing that they share beliefs and a way of life.

- **There are traces of very short creeds in the New Testament.** At the end of his first letter to the Christians at Corinth, Saint Paul writes: "For I handed on to

attested in the *Annals* of Tacitus, a second-century Roman historian). Jesus was raised from the dead, ascended into heaven and will come again as a judge. This is echoed in the acclamation in the eucharist: "Christ has died, Christ is risen, Christ will come again."

The Nicene Creed

We believe in one God,
the Father, the Almighty,
maker of heaven and earth,
of all that is,
seen and unseen.
We believe in one Lord, Jesus Christ,
the only Son of God,
eternally begotten of the Father,
God from God, Light from Light,

true God from true God,
begotten, not made,
of one Being with the Father.
Through him all things were made.
For us and for our salvation
he came down from heaven:
by the power of the Holy Spirit,
he became from the Virgin Mary,
and was made man.
For our sake he was crucified under
*   Pontius Pilate;*
he suffered death and was buried.
On the third day he rose again
in accordance with the Scriptures;
he ascended into heaven
and is seated at the right hand of the
*   Father.*
He will come again in glory to judge
*   the living and the dead,*

you as of first importance what I in turn had received: that Christ died for our sins in accordance with the scriptures, and that he was buried, and that he was raised on the third day in accordance with the scriptures, and that he appeared to Cephas, then to the twelve" (1 Corinthians 15:3-5). Saint Paul says that he has received and handed on something—which is one way of defining *tradition*—and then lists basic beliefs: Christ's death fulfilled scripture; Christ was buried; and Christ was raised from the dead on the third day, to which the disciples gave witness.

- Christians also often produced creeds when they were persecuted. A summary of belief could be used to counter accusations.

- **The most famous creeds date from the fourth and fifth centuries,** when there were violent disagreements between Christians, especially about the nature of Jesus.

- **The Nicene Creed** takes its name from the Council of Nicaea (325 CE), where they debated the question: "In what way was Jesus God and Man?' Arguments about the definition of true belief had become very important because Christianity had become the religion of the Roman Empire after 313 CE. The Nicene Creed is used at the eucharist.

- **The Apostles' Creed** was first known in its present form in about 400 CE. It is used at baptism.

- **Confirmation courses (like this one) are often closely linked to the different parts of the creeds,** just as preparation for baptism (which could last as long as three years, reflecting the fact that baptism was regarded as a very serious step to take) was in the early Church.

and his kingdom will have no end.
We believe in the Holy Spirit,
the Lord, the giver of life,
who proceeds from the Father and the Son.
With the Father and the Son he is
worshiped and glorified.
He has spoken through the Prophets.
We believe in one holy catholic and
apostolic Church.
We acknowledge one baptism for the
forgiveness of sins.

We look for the resurrection of the dead,
and the life of the world to come.
Amen.[3]

Much of the Nicene Creed's language may seem rather technical but its main purpose is to stress that Jesus was truly God and man (see Chapter 2, "Human nature and sin", and Chapter 3, "Jesus: life and ministry").

Thinking it through

- Summarize your own most important beliefs, making them into a creed.

- How can knowing what you believe affect your life?

- Do you think that learning the creeds by heart could be helpful?

- The Stamp Test: Take a piece of paper the size of a stamp. Try writing a motto or phrase to sum up the Christian message that would fit on the back of a stamp.

Bible Study

Read 1 Corinthians 15:1-11.
Saint Paul explains how the gospel has been passed on to him and how he now passes it on to others. He is a most unusual person to be doing this as he himself formerly persecuted Christians. But the grace of God has made him what he is.

- This passage is Paul's statement of belief about Jesus. Turn these verses into a creed.

- Why do you think he mentions that the resurrection (and the teaching

in general) is a matter of public knowledge?

- What does this passage teach about the power of God in an individual life?

FOR PRAYER & REFLECTION

Almighty and everlasting God,
increase in us the gifts of
faith, hope, and charity; and,
that we may obtain what you promise,
make us love what you command;
through Jesus Christ our Lord,
who lives and reigns with you
and the Holy Spirit, one God,
for ever and ever. Amen.[4]

Some prayer **topics**

For a greater understanding of Christian belief.

To experience faith as something personal.

To live the beliefs of the creed.

For courage to stand up for what we believe.

For God's help for those who are persecuted for their beliefs.

Chapter 8
The BIBLE

A powerful book

The Bible is the most widely published and translated book in human history. It has influenced and transformed countless lives.

Some governments, wary of its power, have tried to prevent or restrict its distribution. This is true in North Korea, where simply possessing a Bible is a serious offense. A Christian North Korean was secretly holding a worship service when he heard a knock at his door. Before letting anyone in, he carefully hid his Bible. When he opened the door, three men came into his house and searched it. He was terrified that his Bible would be discovered and that he would be arrested.

Then, one of the men discovered his Bible but—to the Christian's surprise—quickly took it and concealed it, telling the other men that there was nothing suspicious here and that they should go on to the next house.

The next day the man who had concealed the Bible returned and told the surprised Christian that he was also a believer but could not worship with others because of the persecution in the country. He said that God had guided him to the home of a believer, and he was very grateful for this. Returning the Bible, he asked the other man to pray for him.

The Bible has the power to change lives in the direst circumstances. Ernest Gordon, in *Miracle on the River Kwai*, tells of the amazing change that took place in a Japanese prisoner of war camp in Burma. In 1942 the camp was a sea of mud and filth. It was a scene of hard labor and brutal treatment by the guards. There was little food, and every man looked out only for himself. Twelve months later, the ground of the camp was cleared and clean. Huts had been rebuilt and on Christmas morning, 2,000 men were at worship. What had happened?

During the year a prisoner had shared his last crumb of food with another man who was also in desperate need. Then he had died. Among his belongings they found a Bible. Could this be the secret of his life, of his willingness to give to others and not to grasp for himself? One by one the prisoners began to read it. Soon the Spirit of God began to grip their hearts and change their lives.[1]

Love of the Bible has inspired people to take great risks to give people access to it. The photograph shows a Korean translation of the Bible.

Some see the Bible as dangerous

The Bible is dangerous because it has the power to change lives. It has changed more lives than any other book. At its worst, the Bible has been a source of intense disagreements over its meaning to the point of causing wars of religion. At its best, the Bible has inspired self-sacrifice, given meaning to many people's lives, led people to devote a lifetime to its study, and provided the raw material for innumerable works of art.

For example, at an open-air Christian meeting in Chile, when the country was ruled by a dictatorship, a member of the audience approached the speaker after hearing the good news about Jesus. To show his desire to change his way of life, he handed over a suitcase containing a machine gun and a bomb.

A simple sign of the Bible's continued importance can be seen in our courts. When a trial is held and Christian witnesses have to swear to tell the truth, they are first asked to do this on the Holy Bible. This is because Christians see the Bible as the source of the most important truths about life and to swear on it should guarantee that they tell the truth.

The sheer diversity of literature in the Bible is one of the secrets of its continuing popularity through the centuries. There is something for all moods and many different cultures. Its message is not buried in religious jargon only accessible to either believers or scholars, but reflects the issues that people struggle with in daily life. Despite their different emphases, all its authors shared the conviction that this world and its affairs are not just a haphazard sequence of random coincidences, but are the forum of God's activity—a God who (unlike the God of the philosophers) is not remote or unknowable, but a personal being who can be known by ordinary people.

John Drane, Bible scholar[2]

Christian beliefs about the Bible

• **Jesus is the Word of God** (see John 1:1-18) **and the Bible is the primary witness to his life and saving work.** Without it, we would have no reliable information about God's purpose in history or about his Son, Jesus Christ.

• **The books of the Bible were written and collected by people who responded to God's Word** and recorded it for the benefit of those who came after them.

• **The Bible tells the story of how God has spoken and acted in history.** It begins with stories of creation, which teach that the world, its creatures, and human beings are not an accident but willed by God. Human frailty, though, has spoiled the world, but God has a plan to restore it (see "A brief history of God's salvation plan," p. 50).

• **This good news story is historical.** The resurrection is not a science fiction story about a hero whose exploits we enjoy watching on television, nor is it just an interesting idea. As Saint Paul says, "if Christ has not been raised, then our proclamation has been in vain and your faith has been in vain" (1 Corinthians 15:14). For this reason, Christians need to be able to trust the historical evidence in the Bible.

• **The Bible contains interpretation as well as history.** For example, it does not simply tell us about the wanderings of a little-known people—the Israelites—in the Sinai Desert. It also tells us that they were a chosen people and that this was a testing time required by God. In other words, the bare facts are given a context and a meaning. We give things context and meaning all the time, such as when we report something. For example, when the Yitzhak Rabin (then prime minister of Israel) and Yassar Arafat (then Palestinian leader) met each other on the White House lawn in the presence of President Bill Clinton in September 1993, we needed to know that they had been mortal enemies for over forty years to see the significance of their shaking hands. Otherwise, it would have been the unremarkable event of two elderly men greeting each other in a garden. In the same way, if we did not know the context of Jesus' story, all we would know would be this: *Once, there was an idealistic young man who taught the crowds who would listen to him, healed sick people, and ran into trouble with the authorities. After an illegal, secret trial, he underwent a public execution.* Instead, we know that his disciples sensed a unique presence of God in him and that Jesus appeared to them raised from the dead three days after they had fled fearing for their own lives.

• **The full interpretation of the facts took years to develop.** In the different books of the New Testament, we can gradually see the way in which the first Christians came to terms with the facts of Jesus' life. So, from his letters, we may read about the way in which Paul, who had persecuted Jesus, came to believe the gospel and teach the church at Corinth that "in Christ God was reconciling the world to himself, not counting their trespasses against them, and entrusting the message of reconciliation to us" (2 Corinthians 5:19).

A brief history of God's salvation plan

God calls God's people: The Old Testament is the story of the Israelites from Abraham to the period before the coming of Jesus. Its major theme is that God calls God's people—the Israelites—and, though they stray, God never gives up on them, answering their prayers even in the worst of times.

God's covenant with Abraham: God's special relationship with the Israelites began with the covenant with Abraham. Then, when they were in captivity in Egypt, God rescued them for life in the Promised Land, which they reached after their faith had been tested by wandering for forty years in the wilderness of the Sinai Desert.

Living in the Promised Land: Once established in the Promised Land (which many modern Jewish people identify with Israel), they went through many ups and downs in their service of God.

The prophets speak: The prophets spoke out against the Israelites when they strayed from doing God's will and warned them that they would return to captivity if they did not repent.

The Babylonian exile: In 586 BCE, they were driven into exile in Babylon, which led them to question whether God had failed them. The answer given by the prophet Isaiah was that they had failed God. But this did not mean that God would abandon them. If they returned to him, they would be able to rebuild Jerusalem. Connected with this hope was the expectation that a special person, a Messiah, would come to redeem Israel.

The Messiah: God eventually became man to save them, which is the good news (gospel) recorded by the New Testament. This man, Jesus, was rejected by his own people and died a criminal's death. But he was raised from the dead. Jesus' resurrection is the climax of God's work of bringing salvation to humanity.

How to use the Bible in our lives

The Bible is a living book. Christians have always turned to it to understand what God expects of them.

I didn't exactly study the Bible—that great...library of stories, books, letters, songs, unfinished manuscripts, polemics, lists, and lost treasures. Rather, I swam in it. I couldn't read scripture in order to single out one lesson with a beginning, a middle, and an end, or use it to fix a stable doctrine. But in the Bible, The Book of Common Prayer, *and the hymns of many traditions, I discovered something of the spaciousness of God's meaning and the wildness of God's sense of time.*

And I found that Jesus does not, anywhere in the gospels, spend too much time calling his people to have feelings, or ideas, or opinions. He calls us to act: hear these words of mine, and act on them.

Sara Miles, *Jesus Freak*[3]

To make connections between the Bible and the present, many Christians study particular passages of the Bible as members of a Bible study group. How can studying God's Word as a group enhance or expand your understanding?

The Bible was just the means in which I came to know God, it was God that changed my life; in every way possible. I have read it cover to cover only twice; now it's a daily read that I turn to for courage, strength, guidance, and continued knowledge.

Kathleen[4]

These accounts show that there is nothing "out of touch" about the stories of the gospels. They describe many situations, such as when people are sick or suffer, in which it is easy for us to imagine ourselves.

It is important and enjoyable to study the Bible with others. Just as we learn another language best by spending time with people who speak it, so we will learn the language of the Bible best by becoming part of the community of the Church where it is a living language. In the life of the Church, the Bible

has been a living language for almost 2,000 years.

Where to start

The Gospels of Matthew and Luke are probably the best parts of the Bible to begin with as they contain many familiar stories.

After you have spent some time with the Bible, you might consider reading the entire thing. Though some books are harder to read and understand than others, reading the Bible cover to cover provides an understanding of the full expanse of God's Word.

There are many online resources for reading the Bible, understanding it and meditating on the meaning of particular passages. Your priest or parish website will be able to guide you to useful ones. A few worth looking at are:
-forwardmovement.org;
-thecenterforbiblicalstudies.org; and
-Reflections for Daily Prayer app (a Church of England resource). You could also follow the Revised Common Lectionary, which provides readings for every Sunday over a cycle of three years. You simply have to find where you are in the cycle and start from there.

It is useful to have a commentary (a book written by a biblical scholar which helps you to understand what the Bible means) or a set of reader's notes, which are briefer than a commentary. Your priest will be able to suggest useful ones to you.

What to do

- Read a passage. Keep what you choose simple and brief.

- Read a commentary. Discuss it with others (if you are in a group).

• Pray about it.

Be still, then, and know that I am God!
Psalm 46:11

Reading the Bible without meditating on it is like trying to eat without swallowing.
Anonymous

Throughout this book, we have suggested passages at the end of each chapter that will enable you to do this for yourself. By studying the Bible in this way, you will be putting it at the heart of your life as a Christian.

The books themselves

The contents of the Old and New Testaments of the Bible that we know today took more than a century after Jesus' lifetime to be agreed upon. Those books which all Christians accept are said to be "canonical" (from a Greek word for "measure"). They alone measure up to universal standards of historical accuracy and importance.

There has always been some disagreement about another group of books, usually called the Apocrypha (literally meaning "hidden"). They date from the later period of the Old Testament—that is, the time just before Jesus—and are usually printed in Bibles between the Old Testament and the New. They are like books in the back room of a library, which are taken out occasionally but not continually referred to. They have been influential in Christian history but do not have the same status as the canonical Old and New Testaments.

The Old Testament

The Old Testament tells the story of God's dealings with the Jewish people before the time of Jesus. It is the story of how God made a covenant (a promise) with them but how they kept breaking their side of the promise. However, in spite of this, God continued to love them and call them back to him.

The books of the Old Testament, which were originally written in Hebrew, are important because Jesus and the early Christians treated them as having lasting value. In fact, the early Christians had no other Bible but the Jewish one. Also, the point of what Jesus achieved would be lost if we did not have a trustworthy record of what God had done beforehand and the way in which human beings had strayed from God.

The history of the development of the Old Testament is complicated but, basically, the books that are included in it are associated with key figures in Jewish history, like Moses (Exodus), David and Solomon (1 and 2 Samuel; 1 and 2 Kings; 1 and 2 Chronicles) and the prophets (who often have their own books, e.g. Hosea).

The Old Testament was the Bible of Jesus and his followers. The gospels and letters written after Jesus' death and resurrection all assumed familiarity with the Old Testament. This means that we need to know the Old Testament if we are to understand the New Testament. How important this is becomes apparent when you use a Bible with footnotes on each page. Notice how many references there are to the books of the Old Testament.

The Bible is not only to be *read* on our own or in groups. It has always been read aloud in the Christian community to be *heard* by the community.

The New Testament

There is widespread agreement today among Christians about which books should be included in the New Testament. However, for the first few centuries, there was concern about inclusion of certain books, particularly Hebrews, which is anonymous, James, 2 Peter, 2 and 3 John, Jude and Revelation.

The main information about the life of Jesus is found in the four gospels: Matthew, Mark, Luke and John. The Acts of the Apostles tells the story of the spread of the gospel and the founding of the first Christian communities. The letters reveal more about those communities and the efforts of their leaders, especially Saint Paul, to apply the gospel to everyday life. The book of

Revelation uses vivid language to describe a vision of the end of time.

The Bible in prayer and church services

When you go to church services, you will often hear psalms from the Old Testament sung just as they are written there, or adapted into hymns or choruses.

Usually, passages from the Old and New Testaments will be read to the congregation and explained in sermons.

In the eucharist, the central prayer recalling the Lord's Supper is taken virtually unchanged from the New Testament. Many of the formal prayers used are based on quotations from the Bible.

Thinking it through

- Why can the Bible be seen as a dangerous book?

- Why does the Bible matter so much to Christians?

- Why do Christians trust the Bible?

- Choose a passage from the Bible that is important for you. Explain to the other members of your group why you value it.

Bible Study

Read the parable of the Vineyard (Mark 12:1-11), which summarizes the outline of God's involvement with humanity.

In this story the owner is God, the people of Israel the first tenants, the servants his prophets, the son Jesus, and the people to whom the vineyard is ultimately given the Gentiles (non-Jews).

- What does this story teach us about God's nature?

- How could this story be seen as warning people not to be complacent about having God's favor?

- In what ways do you feel that we can be like the tenants who were reluctant to pay their rent?

FOR PRAYER & REFLECTION

Blessed Lord,
who caused all holy Scriptures to be
*   written for our learning:*
Grant us so to hear them, read, mark,
*   learn, and inwardly digest them,*
that we may embrace and ever hold fast
*   the blessed hope of everlasting life,*
which you have given us in our Savior
*   Jesus Christ;*
who lives and reigns with you and the
*   Holy Spirit,*
one God, for ever and ever. Amen.[5]

Some prayer **topics**

Ask for God's help in understanding the Bible.

Pray to hear God's Word for yourself through the reading of the Bible.

Ask for help for those who have difficulty obtaining Bibles or are persecuted for owning them.

Chapter 9

LIVING as a CHRISTIAN

Grant to us, Lord, we pray, the spirit to think and do always those things that are right, that we, who cannot exist without you, may by you be enabled to live according to your will.

—*The Book of Common Prayer, p. 232*

Change is a fundamental human experience. As we grow up, we move from one school to another and often we move houses. To cope with these moves, we have to adapt and change.

Being a Christian should change the sort of person you are. Not in some holier-than-thou, goody-goody way. But Christians should be people who:

• are willing to talk about their faith;

• go out of their way to serve other people;

• forgive others;

• encourage those who are at odds to forgive one another.

In short, Christians are the companions and followers of Jesus and should live in a way he would approve of. They are also mindful that the way they act now will affect the way in which they are judged in the life to come.

Innumerable books have been written about how to live as a Christian, but certain ideas crop up in all of them. Important ones are:

conscience, forgiveness, judgment, and a belief that God notices everything that we do.

Conscience

Even small children rapidly develop a sense of right and wrong. As they grow older, they usually become more sophisticated in their ability to reason about moral decisions. This capacity to reason about the right course of action is called *conscience*. We use the word conscience in a number of revealing ways. We talk about someone who takes care as being *conscientious*. People who have done something wrong have a *guilty conscience* and those who have behaved well will declare that they have a *clear conscience*.

Christians use their conscience properly when they consider the options available to them in the light of scripture and tradition and through the guidance of the Holy Spirit.

In practice, this means that we need to take part in a parish life where the Christian tradition is alive and where it is normal to discuss and pray about moral decisions.

Repentance and forgiveness

Then Peter came to Jesus and said to him, "Lord, if another member of the church sins against me, how often should I forgive? As many as seven times?"

Jesus said to him, "Not seven times, but, I tell you, seventy-seven times."

Matthew 18:21-22

Part of being human is that we all do things wrong and stand in need of forgiveness. Forgiveness is one of the most distinctive features of Christianity. Jesus himself forgave those who crucified him: "Father, forgive them; for they do not know what they are doing" (Luke 23:34). He also taught about forgiveness in parables, the most famous of which is the parable of the Prodigal (Lost) Son (Luke 15:11-32). In this parable, the younger of two sons asked his father for his inheritance. He went away to a distant land and wasted the money in loose living. Eventually, he was reduced to feeding pigs for a living, even eating their food. After a time, he thought he would fare better if he returned home as a servant in his father's house. By doing this, he repented. To his surprise, his father was looking out for him, and on his return embraced him with enthusiasm and ordered a celebratory meal to be prepared. In this story, the father represents God rejoicing at the repentance of a sinner.

Repentance literally means turning around or changing direction. It opens us to receiving forgiveness. Being forgiven helps us to rebuild our lives and start growing again. This isn't something that will happen only occasionally. We will find ourselves repenting and needing forgiveness over and over again.

Being virtuous doesn't preclude slipping up and falling, once in a while. Being virtuous means getting up and trying again.

Michel Quoist[1]

God helped me to learn to forgive—the most difficult of all lessons. It didn't happen in a day and it wasn't easy. But I finally got it.

Kim is best known as the girl (middle left) in this famous photo of a Vietnam War napalm-bombing attack near Saigon. She now lives in Toronto with her husband and two children. Her organization, Kim Foundation International, aids children who are war victims.

Forgiveness made me free from hatred. I still have many scars on my body and severe pain most days but my heart is cleansed.

Napalm is very powerful but faith, forgiveness, and love are much more powerful. We would not have war at all if everyone could learn how to live with true love, hope and forgiveness.

Kim Phuc[2]

Judgment

New Testament teaching about judgment provides a counterbalance to that about forgiveness.

A famous story (John 8:3-11) illustrates this. A woman had been caught committing adultery. Her accusers brought her before Jesus, expecting to exact the usual punishment of death by stoning. Jesus' response was to ask the person who had never sinned to cast the first stone. Since none could claim to be without sin, they all slipped away, the oldest, with the longest life in which to have sinned, being the first to go. Jesus was left facing the woman. He told her to go away and sin no more.

The interesting point about this story is that Jesus does not treat the woman as if she had not sinned. Nor does he make her forgiveness depend upon her repentance. He simply warns her not to repeat her sin.

From this Christians recognize that God judges our wrong acts. But God also forgives us and expects us to be free to change our lives once we are forgiven.

God sees everything

Truly I tell you, just as you did not do it to one of the least of these, you did not do it to me.

Matthew 25:45

The parable of the Sheep and the Goats (Matthew 25:31-46) gives a famous illustration of the way in which God notices all our good and evil acts and how important it is to respond to the needs of those who suffer.

Jesus describes a judgment that resembles the way in which a shepherd in the Holy Land separates sheep from goats (unlike the breeds familiar to us, these animals in biblical times were quite similar to the inexperienced eye). God judges as good all those who have fed the hungry, given refreshment to the thirsty, welcomed the stranger, clothed the needy, and visited the sick and those in prison. The bad are all those who have ignored these needs.

The remarkable feature of the story is that Jesus sees all these good acts as having been done to him and all the times when people have neglected to do them as a failure of love toward him.

This means that Christians should see Jesus as being at the heart of all their moral decisions. In a way, we should ask ourselves this simple question when faced with a moral problem: *Is this what I would do to Jesus?*

Who is my neighbor?

The parable of the Sheep and the Goats should be coupled with that of the

The Church and morality

- For Episcopalians, making moral decisions is a threefold process: Anglicans summarize the decision-making process by saying that we have a threefold approach to making moral decisions: we appeal to scripture, tradition, and reason.

  1 We first seek guidance from what the Bible teaches;

  2 we look to see how previous generations of Christians have interpreted biblical teaching;

  3 while doing this, we use the human faculty of reason, which distinguishes us from other creatures. It entails the prayerful use of our minds to discover what we should do with the help of the Spirit.

- The teaching or guidance of the bishops: An important contribution to this process comes from the teaching of our bishops, who have the responsibility to preserve and interpret tradition. So, when there is a difficult moral question—about divorce and remarriage, stem-cell research, or same-sex relationships— the bishops study and debate the issue and publish their conclusions.

However, the bishops' teaching in the Anglican Church does not claim the same level of authority as that asserted for papal teaching within the Roman Catholic Church. The aim of the bishops' teaching is to offer guidance to Anglicans and especially to priests in helping individuals who seek their moral advice. This leaves space for individual conscience and often gives rise to a diversity of moral views among Anglicans.

Sometimes, the bishops' guidance comes not simply from the House of Bishops of the Episcopal Church but from the bishops of all the Anglican churches worldwide (known as the Anglican Communion). Since 1867, the bishops of the Anglican Communion have held conferences, called Lambeth Conferences after the Archbishop of Canterbury's London home where they first met. These conferences are held every ten years to discuss the most important questions facing Anglicans. An example of their teaching is the approval they expressed for the practice of artificial contraception, which has been permissible for Anglicans since the Lambeth Conference of 1930.

Good Samaritan (Luke 10:25-37). In the parable of the Sheep and Goats, anyone in need deserves our help. The Good Samaritan parable makes a similar point.

A lawyer asked Jesus, "Who is my neighbor?" Jesus replied by telling the story of a man who had been mugged and left for dead. Two people of high social standing, a Levite and a priest, passed him by. Only a Samaritan, who belonged to a minority group looked down upon by Jesus' contemporaries, helped the injured man and arranged for him to be looked after. The lawyer, said Jesus, should "Go, and do likewise."

This parable implies that anyone we come across can be seen as our "neighbor" and deserving of our help. Christians should not be concerned only

Living as a Christian often means that we have to speak out or take action on issues of social justice. Members of Holy Faith Episcopal Church in Inglewood, California, lead demonstrators in one of several chants, calling for immigration reform and justice for all.

with their immediate families, friends and neighbors. Even strangers should be seen as neighbors. Such teaching underlies Christian appeals to provide help for people abroad or those in our society with whom we have no "neighborly" contact in the narrow sense of the people we know.

A change of character

We could sum up the whole of Christian moral teaching as a desire to have our character and attitude changed by God so that we are different in ourselves and in our behavior toward others.

Whether I behave toward someone else as I would toward Jesus is less a matter of keeping to certain rules and more to do with a change of character. Christians believe that this can happen through the Holy Spirit working in the depth of our personalities, changing our whole way of seeing things and our behavior.

Our ancestors have said that we should cultivate the seven great virtues: wisdom, fortitude, temperance, justice, faith, hope, and love. We could draw up a simpler list to begin with. Christians should show honesty, thoughtfulness, sensitivity, and compassion toward others. Or, to use other words, we should have integrity and exercise responsibility. In the Bible Peter provides a list of qualities that Christians should cultivate: goodness, knowledge, self-control, endurance, godliness, mutual affection, and love (2 Peter 1:5-7).

Christian community

- One name for the community is the kingdom of God. It is united by belief and sharing of communion. The kingdom of God may be depicted as a banquet to which all are invited and where those who push for a better deal for themselves will be expected to give way to the humble.

- Forgiveness characterizes this community. Jesus himself had time for the outcasts of his day—tax collectors, adulterers, and prostitutes. Since tax collectors made their living by collecting money for the hated Roman occupiers of Palestine and the penalty for adultery was death, his befriending of them was remarkable.

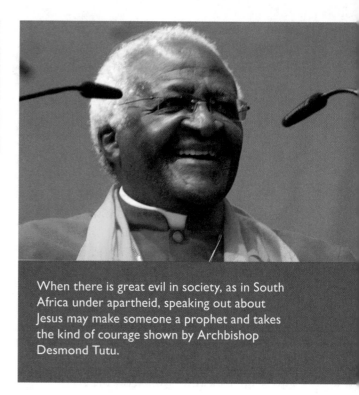

When there is great evil in society, as in South Africa under apartheid, speaking out about Jesus may make someone a prophet and takes the kind of courage shown by Archbishop Desmond Tutu.

Christian beliefs about how to live

- Christians are to love God and love their neighbors as themselves. There is no system of laws which Christians have to obey. However, there is the Great Commandment to love God and to love your neighbor as yourself. This provides a framework within which all Christian teaching about moral decisions falls. The Ten Commandments (see Exodus 20:2-17) also provide an essential framework, condemning killing, theft, and adultery in particular.

A Christian society will be one where everyone is welcome regardless of their social status or origins. As Saint Paul wrote, "For in the one Spirit we were all baptized into one body—Jews or Greeks, slaves or free" (1 Corinthians 12:13). See the "Christian community" panel above.

- Christians are to feel special moral obligations toward those who are ill, poor, or excluded from society. A core part of Christian moral thinking and practice concerns those whom Jesus particularly valued: the poor, the outcast, and the sick. It is natural for Christians to campaign for political and social action. The involvement of the Anglican Church in South Africa in the effort to end apartheid is a good example of this.

- The Holy Spirit is always at hand to help us to make moral decisions. The name "tradition" is given to the accumulated experience of the insights that the Holy Spirit has given generations of Christians. However, we should not apply tradition unthinkingly. In order to discern what to do, we need to reason and pray about what tradition teaches and also take account of biblical teaching (see "The Church and morality" section, p. 58).

Thinking it through

- If someone asked you to summarize what "living as a Christian" meant, what would you say?

- How much should we be prepared to forgive others?

- Why should Christians be concerned for the welfare of others, even those they do not know?

- How do we discover in practice what it is right to do?

- Should our Christian beliefs affect the way we vote?

Bible Study

Read Jesus' teaching about forgiveness in the Sermon on the Mount (Matthew 5:38-48).

Here Jesus is urging his followers to adopt an entirely different standard from those who would merely "pay back" the harm done to them. He expects his disciples to show as much forgiveness and goodness as God does.

- What attitude is represented by "an eye for an eye?"

- Is Jesus' teaching too high an ideal?

- How might a Christian be helped in trying to practice this teaching?

- How do we expect Jesus to treat us if we fail to live up to his standard of forgiveness?

FOR PRAYER & REFLECTION

This great prayer about peace and forgiveness is often attributed to Saint Francis of Assisi.

> *Lord, make us instruments of your peace.*
> *Where there is hatred, let us sow love;*
> *where there is injury, let there be pardon;*
> *where there is discord, union;*
> *where there is doubt, faith;*
> *where there is despair, hope;*
> *where there is darkness, light;*
> *where there is sadness, joy;*
> *for your mercy and for your truth's sake.*
> *Amen.*[3]

Some prayer **topics**

Ask for God's forgiveness for those things we regret doing.

Pray for help from God in understanding how to know and act upon God's will.

Ask for help to be able to forgive others.

Pray for the strength to do something to relieve the suffering of those we do not know personally.

Chapter 10

PRAYER and WORSHIP

How do I pray?

A young man is dying of cancer. He is so weak that he can no longer climb the stairs, and his family has made a bedroom downstairs for him. He has been asking his older brother whether he is going to get better and his brother has broken the news to him that he is going to die.

A priest comes to visit, and the young man asks him how to pray, as he has never really prayed very much and isn't sure how to go about it.

The priest says that it is like having a conversation. Just say to God what you feel. Tell God about your pain and tiredness, about your worries for your family and how they are going to cope after you've died. Tell God about all the things you feel sorry about and regret as you look back over your life. Ask God for help.

The young man seems to understand this, but he asks again whether there are some special words he can use. The priest suggests that they say the Lord's Prayer together. It is very moving to see the young man with great simplicity put his frail hands together and say "Our Father" in little more than a whisper. For his remaining days, he is very calm, and on the night before he dies, he is able to say goodbye to his whole family.

Most people are moved to prayer at the important moments of their lives. Confronted by illness, difficulties with family or friendships, major exams, or other big problems, it seems natural to cry out to God. But we can also be moved to prayer by great beauty.

Standing on top of a mountain on a clear day and contemplating the wonder of the created world, we feel awe at the majesty and beauty of the view.

In fact, on any occasion when we are lifted out of the ordinary, whether we feel pain or joy, we want to express it, not just to other people, but to God.

The ways in which we do this are as varied as the ways in which we speak. We may pray to God speaking as simply as we would to members of our family. When we do this, we are following Jesus' teaching that we should address God as 'Our Father'.

At other times, we may find set words a help. If we are feeling very emotional, set words may provide us with something solid to hold on to and channel our thoughts and feelings. Or they can help when we don't know what words to begin with.

Like other kinds of communication, prayer needs practice. We learn to speak, read, and write by endless repetition and practice. Prayer becomes natural if we pray frequently and regularly.

Prayer, like conversation, is a two-way process. We need to listen to God as well as speak to God. Also, just as we sometimes have one-to-one conversations, and at other times we are talking in the company of many others, so Christians also pray to God with other people. This is what happens in church services and in prayer groups.

When you have a great friend you may plan to spend a time with him and may be careful not to miss it. The use of the time is unlikely to be planned, but within the time news may be shared, requests may be made, regrets or gratitude may be spoken, and minds may be changed sometimes by talking and

People may find a particular posture helpful when praying. Which posture do you find most helpful?

listening and sometimes with a little word or gesture...May not our prayer be rather like that?

Michael Ramsey[1]

Types of prayer

I pray because I can't help myself. I pray because I'm helpless, I pray because the need flows out of me all the time, waking and sleeping. It doesn't change God, it changes me.

C. S. Lewis[2]

The main kinds of Christian prayer are adoration, confession, thanksgiving, and supplication. They are often remembered by the abbreviation ACTS.

Adoration
"To be with God wondering"[3]

As we look around at the world, there is so much to praise God for. The world with its beauty and majesty can make you stand in awe and wonder. The view from a high mountain, the force of a great storm, the intricate beauty of plants, or the delicate mechanism of the human body are all capable of stimulating a sense of awe. This can make us want to offer a prayer of adoration to God, the source of the "awe-full" things. Sometimes, the sense of awe can be so great that we feel very small and humble, even terrified. Perhaps you feel this staring at a vast landscape from the top of a high mountain or from an airplane. This was the original sense of the word "awful," which is often overused and has lost much of its original force.

Confession
"To be with God ashamed"

Praying isn't always nice. When we do wrong we need to face up to what we have done and ask God to forgive us. As we know from the parable of the Prodigal Son and many other parts of Jesus' teaching, God wants to forgive everybody. But God also wants us to change (repent), which can be very hard.

> *People think that when Christians pray we just get a nice cozy feeling inside. There is nothing very cozy about standing before your Maker.*
> Natalie, 15 (quoted in Carrie Mercier)[4]

Thanksgiving
"To be with God gratefully"

We all have so much to thank God for—our health, our security, our family, and friends. In offering God prayers of thanksgiving, we are saying how grateful we are.

One of the most famous set prayers of thanksgiving is the General Thanksgiving in *The Book of Common Prayer,* which has been in regular use since the sixteenth century:

> *Almighty God, Father of all mercies, we thine unworthy servants do give thee most humble and hearty thanks for all thy goodness and loving-kindness to us...*

The Church's current prayer book provides a set of Thanksgivings to be used at Morning and Evening Prayer.

At the end of the eucharist, we also say a prayer of thanksgiving for receiving communion:

> *Almighty God and everliving God,*
> *   we thank you for feeding us*
> *with the spiritual food of the most precious*
> *   Body and Blood of your Son*
> *   our Savior Jesus Christ;*
> *and for assuring us in these holy mysteries*
> *that we are living members of the*
> *   Body of your Son,*
> *and heirs of your eternal kingdom.*
> *And now, Father, send us out*
> *to do the work you have given us to do,*
> *to love and serve you*
> *as faithful witnesses of Christ our Lord.*
> *To him, to you, and to the Holy Spirit,*
> *be honor and glory, now and for ever.*
> *   Amen.*[5]

Supplication
"To be with God, with others in mind, that is intercession"

Jesus told his disciples, "Ask, and it will be given to you; search, and you will find; knock, and the door will be opened for you" (Matthew 7:7). In prayer we should not only pray for our own needs but also for the needs of others. This is called intercession. By doing this we are not trying to twist God's arm to make him do things. We are joining with God in the spiritual battle God is waging against evil, against all that tries to destroy good. Intercessory prayer can be very demanding—it takes effort to put yourself in the position of another person, to think about what that person may be feeling, feel his or her pain, and offer it up to God to work in the person's situation. But our intercessory prayers for others must not take the place of action. God may well be asking us to do something about the situation. In this we need to seek God's guidance.

Styles of worship

If you went to a communion service in a hospital you would not expect it to be the same as a grand service with a professional choir in a cathedral. Different places and occasions call for different styles of worship and levels of formality.

But there is also variety in the Episcopal Church that stems from differences of belief and attitude. At the time of the Reformation in the sixteenth century, some people would have liked to see the Church of England become more Protestant and others regretted that it could not have remained Roman Catholic.

The history since then is very involved but as a broad generalization, this tension has remained in the Church of England, carried over into the Episcopal Church, and throughout much of the worldwide Anglican Communion. Those of a more "Low" approach (i.e. having a lower view of the importance of bishops, priesthood, and sacraments) tend to prefer simpler worship and those of a more (often called "Anglo-Catholic") "High" approach (i.e. those who value bishops, priesthood, and sacraments highly) prefer more elaborate

Special vestments, like uniforms, are worn for formal worship. Here, the acolytes (holding the candles) are wearing albs while the priest wears a stole (or scarf).

services, with beautiful vestments, choral singing, and incense.

Sometimes there is vigorous controversy between the different approaches, but many Episcopalians are glad that our Church is broad enough to include such variety. You may well find that you are happy to move around sampling different styles. Often whether we prefer one style or another depends upon our temperament and what we are used to.

The Christian calendar

Christians remind themselves of the main parts of Christian teaching by observing an annual cycle of seasons and festivals called the Christian calendar. The birth of Jesus is recalled at Christmas; his temptations in the

Christian beliefs about prayer and worship

- **When a Christian prays, he or she stands before God.** In prayer we open our minds and hearts to God. We do not have to hide anything from God, we can be completely open with God: if we are sad, we share that with God; if we are angry, we need to share that too.

- **Worship is the heart of all prayer.** When we worship someone, we mean that we place great worth on that person, acknowledging his or her "worthship." Christians base their approach to prayer and worship on what Jesus did.

- **Praying regularly and frequently is beneficial.** The New Testament shows us that Jesus prayed frequently and set aside special times to pray. The gospels tell us that Jesus often woke early and went away to a quiet place to spend time alone with God. At other times, he would go to the synagogue (the Jewish place of worship) to join in communal prayer and worship. The Christian practice of regular prayer (the clergy pray twice a day at least, and monks and nuns more frequently) and meeting in church for worship reflects Jesus' life. Whenever he had a big decision to make, Jesus prayed. Just before he was betrayed by Judas, he prayed in the Garden of Gethsemane, asking God whether he should "drink the cup of suffering" and die. "Abba, Father," he said, "for you all things are possible; remove this cup from me; yet, not what I want, but what you want."

- **Prayer helps believers to understand and do God's will, as Jesus did.** This is the main purpose of prayer. Jesus prayed to God as a son speaks to his father, asking only to do his will. To do God's will, we have to listen to God. There is an old Christian saying that "God has given you two ears and one mouth that you may listen twice as much as you speak to God."

- **In prayer, we should open our hearts and minds to God just as Jesus did.** There is no need to hide anything from him. We can reveal sadness, joy and anger to him. In fact, Jesus teaches us that our God "knows what you need before you ask him."

- **We are not on our own as we pray.** The Holy Spirit helps us. As Saint Paul writes, "the Spirit helps us in our weakness; for we do not know how to pray as we ought" (Romans 8:26).

- **Christians need both private and public prayer and worship.** When we pray and worship on our own, we are building up our individual relationship with God. But, as Christians, we are part of the Church, often called "the Body of Christ" or "the People of God," and we support one another by praying and worshiping together. Just as in the life of a well-ordered family, we need times on our own and times together.

- **Setting time aside to be with God helps a person to gain perspective on life.** Today everyone is so busy and rushed that it is easy to get caught up in the rat race. Prayer provides time for us to try to see things the way God sees them, to endeavor to see the world through God's eyes.

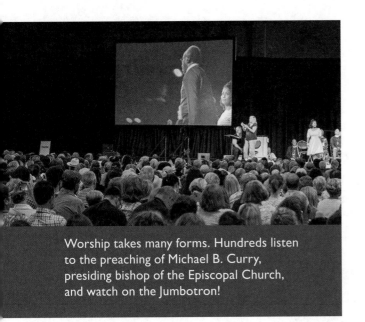

Worship takes many forms. Hundreds listen to the preaching of Michael B. Curry, presiding bishop of the Episcopal Church, and watch on the Jumbotron!

(though some churches have a Lenten Array made of unbleached linen); red for Pentecost and martyrs; and green for the rest of the year.

A practical approach to prayer and worship

- Anyone can start praying at any time, but don't be afraid to ask someone experienced to help you. Ask your priest or youth leader for advice.

- You should try to establish a habit of prayer and worship. As with everything else, commitment and practice help. Try to pray every day (even if only very briefly) and go to church every week (for most people this will be on a Sunday).

wilderness in Lent; his entry into Jerusalem, the Last Supper, crucifixion and resurrection at Easter; his Ascension and the gift of the Holy Spirit creating the Church at Ascension and Pentecost. We also commemorate the Holy Trinity on the Sunday after Pentecost and other events in the life of Jesus, Mary, the apostles, and saints on a variety of feast and saints' days.

Many ceremonies and customs associated with these special days. For example, at Christmas we sing carols; during Lent Christians give up something to commemorate Jesus' fast for forty days in the wilderness; on Palm Sunday we carry palms in procession; on Good Friday the cross is honored; and a bonfire and Paschal (Easter) candle are lit to mark the resurrection on Holy Saturday evening.

The vestments worn by the clergy and the frontals (coverings on the front of the altars) change according to the season of the Church's calendar. White or gold is used for festivals of Jesus, Mary, and the saints (apart from the martyrs); purple is used for Advent and Lent

Do I have to go to church to be a Christian?

A man was invited to a meal by his friend, a priest. When they had eaten, they began talking about prayer and the man asked the priest whether it was necessary to pray and worship with other people. Instead of replying with an argument, the priest told the man to watch what he did. He leaned forward, picked up the tongs and removed a red-hot coal from the fire. It gradually became dark and cool. Then he replaced it among the other lumps of coal. Quickly it became hot and bright again, and the whole fire burned slightly brighter.

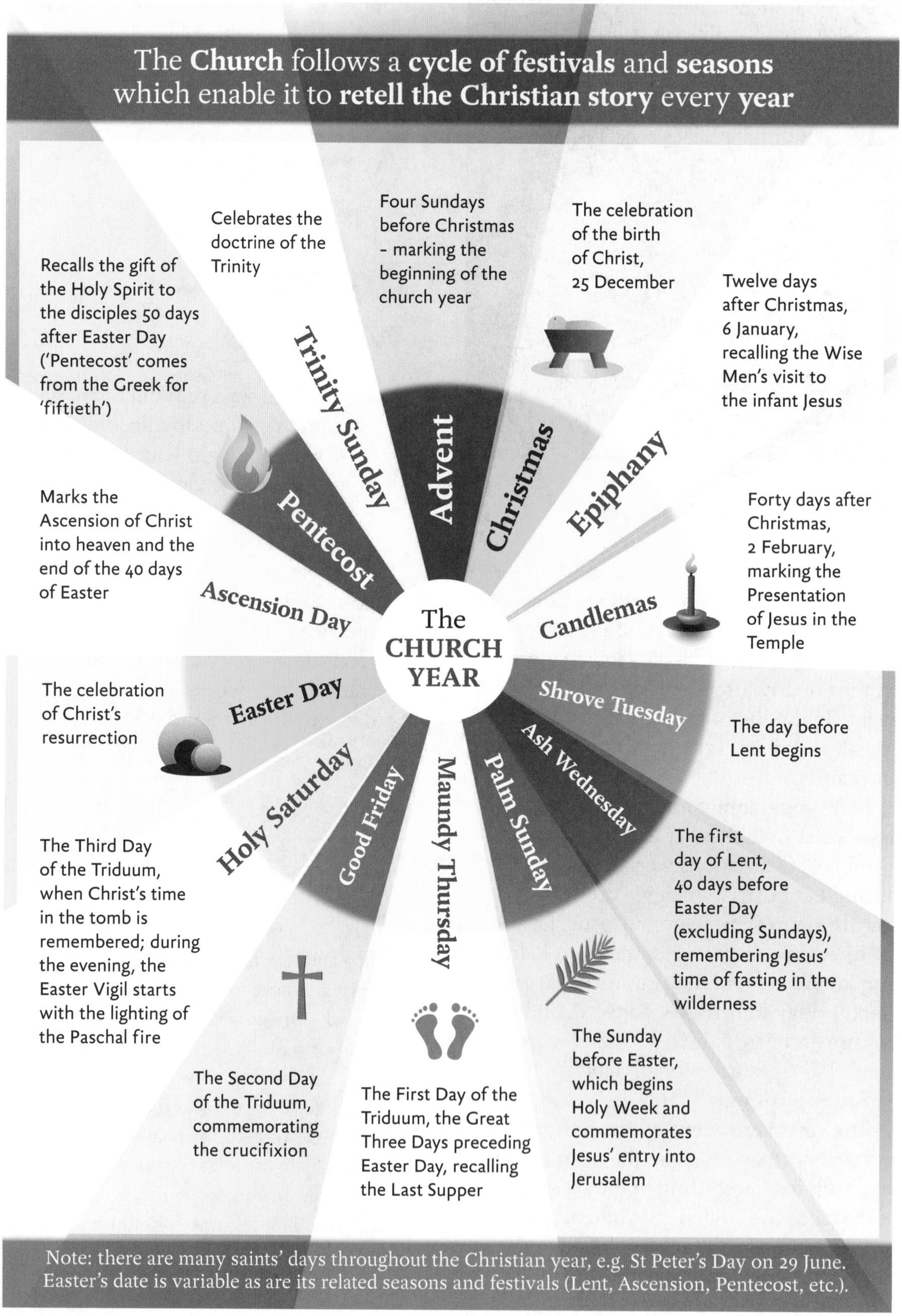

The **Church** follows a **cycle of festivals** and **seasons** which enable it to **retell the Christian story** every **year**

Celebrates the doctrine of the Trinity

Four Sundays before Christmas - marking the beginning of the church year

The celebration of the birth of Christ, 25 December

Recalls the gift of the Holy Spirit to the disciples 50 days after Easter Day ('Pentecost' comes from the Greek for 'fiftieth')

Twelve days after Christmas, 6 January, recalling the Wise Men's visit to the infant Jesus

Marks the Ascension of Christ into heaven and the end of the 40 days of Easter

Forty days after Christmas, 2 February, marking the Presentation of Jesus in the Temple

Trinity Sunday

Advent

Christmas

Epiphany

Pentecost

Ascension Day

Candlemas

The CHURCH YEAR

Easter Day

Shrove Tuesday

Ash Wednesday

The day before Lent begins

The celebration of Christ's resurrection

Holy Saturday

Good Friday

Maundy Thursday

Palm Sunday

The first day of Lent, 40 days before Easter Day (excluding Sundays), remembering Jesus' time of fasting in the wilderness

The Third Day of the Triduum, when Christ's time in the tomb is remembered; during the evening, the Easter Vigil starts with the lighting of the Paschal fire

The Second Day of the Triduum, commemorating the crucifixion

The First Day of the Triduum, the Great Three Days preceding Easter Day, recalling the Last Supper

The Sunday before Easter, which begins Holy Week and commemorates Jesus' entry into Jerusalem

Note: there are many saints' days throughout the Christian year, e.g. St Peter's Day on 29 June. Easter's date is variable as are its related seasons and festivals (Lent, Ascension, Pentecost, etc.).

- Experiment with different styles of service so that you find what works best for you at the moment. But bear in mind that this may change as time goes by.

- To begin praying we need to be still and silent. If we are quiet, we can hear God. Praying involves listening to God as well as speaking to God.

- While belonging to a worshiping community helps us to keep going with prayer (see the story on p. 67), there will be times when we will want, or have, to pray alone. No one apart from God needs to know that you are praying. You can be sitting on a train, going to work or school, and you can still pray.

I remember taking a service in Oxford Prison and having to give a talk at rather short notice. I spoke about how we could pray without anyone knowing. I was aware that many of the inmates listening would find it very difficult if their fellows knew that they were praying. (Obviously, they wouldn't be able to kneel by their beds at night, like a small child saying its prayers.) So I said that they could just be lying on their bunks first thing in the morning or last thing at night, when everyone else was asleep, and still pray quietly to God.

A friend of mine, who was the prison chaplain, visited the prison the next day. One of the young men he spoke to had just had an appendicitis operation and was feeling very low and depressed. He told my friend what a difference it had made to him to hear "that bloke we had yesterday" saying that you could pray so simply that no one else even needed to know.

A parish priest

Lighting candles or other outward gestures often accompany and assist prayer. We find it helpful to do something outward to express what is happening inwardly. The light of a candle can also help us to concentrate when we pray.

- Some practical things can help you to pray, though. Set prayers, especially if you memorize them, can give you something to repeat aloud or to yourself to settle the mind. You can use the Lord's Prayer in this way, praying it slowly, line by line, with pauses for meditation in between. You might also use one of the collects (see the "Origin of the collects" section, p. 70).

- You may like to choose a room or place where you can be quiet. Some people have a cross or picture of Jesus to focus on when they begin praying. Or perhaps they light a candle and focus on it as they pray. Obviously, your church or a chapel within it could be a good place if it's easy to get to and open regularly. But you will also want to establish a place in your own home and a time when it is convenient.

- The way you sit or kneel can help, especially if you are going to pray for some time. Try sitting upright in a chair that allows your feet to touch the ground. Rest your hands on the armrests or on your knees. Breathe slowly in and out, becoming aware of your breathing as you pray. (There are many guides to prayer which go into far more detail than we can here.) You may also find it helpful to use a rosary to order your meditation.

- If you pray with others in a group, you will be able to help one another.

Origin of the collects

The word "collect" originally meant a prayer collecting together separate prayers from different members of a congregation into one. Today there are special collects each Sunday, which "collect" together the themes of the readings for that day into one prayer. The same is done for saints' days.

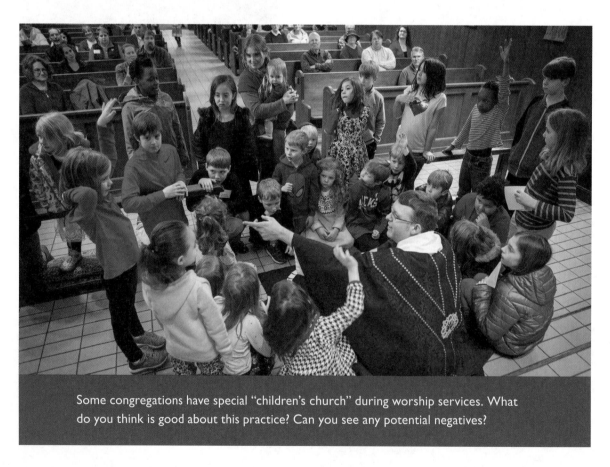

Some congregations have special "children's church" during worship services. What do you think is good about this practice? Can you see any potential negatives?

Thinking it through

- Which time do you think would be the best to set aside for prayer?

- What do you think you are doing when you pray?

- What does it mean to listen to God in prayer? How does God speak to people? Do you expect to hear a voice or does God communicate through other means?

- How would you respond to someone who said that God does not answer prayer because God does not heal everyone who is sick and prays?

- C. S. Lewis said he prayed because he needed to. What do you think he meant? Do you agree with him?

FOR PRAYER & REFLECTION

Almighty and everlasting God,
you are always more ready to hear than
*   we to pray*
and to give more than either we desire or
*   deserve:*
pour down upon us the abundance of your
*   mercy,*
forgiving us those things of which our
*   conscience is afraid*
and giving us those good things which we
*   are not worthy to ask. Amen.*[6]

Bible Study

Read Matthew 6:9-13.

Matthew's Gospel provides the longer version of the Lord's Prayer. Apart from being the most famous Christian prayer, it also reminds us of the need to pray simply.

Some prayer **topics**

Ask God to help you pray.

Pray through a newspaper. Carefully select two or three articles to read. After each one, take time to reflect prayerfully on people in the story—offer each person up to God. Also learn to pray over the TV news—offer up quick prayers as you watch.

Go through the past week in your mind and thank God for all that has happened. "Lord, teach us to worship you throughout the day."

Chapter 11
The SACRAMENTS

What is a sacrament?

A sacrament is symbolic

The term *body language* is used to describe the way people communicate with one another in non-verbal ways, by using facial expressions, body postures, and eye movements. Humans use their bodies to communicate inner meanings—how they think and feel. Much of the body language we use is symbolic. These gestures help us to express ourselves when we find it difficult to put our feelings and thoughts into words.

For Christians, the sacraments provide special ceremonies and gestures that enable us to communicate our deepest religious thoughts and feelings at key moments in our lives.

A sacrament points to God

Have you noticed how many advertisements are shot in lavish locations? They are designed to suggest that if you buy the product, you too can enjoy a world of luxury. The product becomes a symbol pointing to something else.

In a way, the same is the case with a sacrament. A sacrament should not just be seen from the outside. It should also be seen as pointing to something else hidden inside, at the spiritual level. So, in the sacrament of the eucharist, the bread and wine looked at from the outside are simply bread and wine, but from the inside, they also point to the presence of Christ in the world.

Everything is, or can become, sacramental. For Saint Francis of Assisi, for example, everything spoke of

God—the lambs in the field, the flowers, even fire and death. The whole world became a sacrament pointing to God.

If everything can be sacramental, we might well ask why the Church has a limited number of sacraments.

The answer is that each of the Church's sacraments celebrate a turning point in a person's life.

Anglicans don't always agree on the number of sacraments. During the Reformation in the 1500 and 1600s, the Church focused on two sacraments: baptism and eucharist. Later on, in the nineteenth century especially, Anglicans began to talk about seven sacraments. Today, we traditionally divide the sacraments into two categories. The dominical sacraments (taught by Jesus) are baptism and eucharist. The five ecclesial sacraments (taught by the church) are confirmation, healing (unction), reconciliation (confession), marriage, and ordination. Our *Book of Common Prayer* is somewhat inconsistent but usually calls the first two "sacraments" and the last five "sacramental rites." In terms of our theology all seven are sacramental: They are outward and visible signs of inward and spiritual grace.

The two parts of a sacrament

1 A visible part—something material is used in a sacrament. For example, water is poured over the candidate's forehead at baptism; bread and wine are consumed at the eucharist; oil is used for the anointing of the sick. The material things focus on the reality of God's presence in a uniquely appropriate way: water in baptism expresses the washing away of sin; the bread and wine of the eucharist express the body and blood of Jesus.

2 The spiritual or invisible part—God comes close to the worshiper through the physical elements. In each sacrament God gives the Holy Spirit to encourage and strengthen us in a particular way.

The seven sacraments

* Baptism

* Confirmation

* Eucharist

* Marriage

* Confession

* Ordination

* Anointing the sick

Baptism and the eucharist are the sacraments that Jesus commanded his disciples to continue, while the other five are sacraments taught by the church. Each of the seven sacraments is explained in detail in the following chapters.

Christian beliefs about the sacraments

- Sacraments are central to the worship of the Church. In the earliest tradition of the Church, the word *sacrament* was used for anything related to the sacred, to everything that was believed to make the holy present. In the twelfth century, the Church pinpointed seven sacraments. They are ceremonies or rituals: Two can be traced back to the time of Jesus (baptism and the eucharist); the other five can be traced back to the early Church (confirmation, confession, marriage, ordination, and anointing of the sick).

- A sacrament is an outward sign of an invisible, spiritual reality. The best-known definition of a sacrament is that given by Saint Augustine (354-430 CE): "A sacrament is the visible form of an invisible grace." Today, we often say that sacraments are "outward and visible signs of inward or spiritual grace." Another way of defining a sacrament is to say that it is a signpost pointing to God, or a dramatization of something that is happening spiritually within a person. As both of these definitions indicate, there are two parts to a sacrament.

- It is important to have a right attitude when receiving the gift of the sacraments:. We should not regard them as magic. We have to receive them believing in the gift that God is giving us through them.

- The sacraments express important developments and changes in a person's life. Entry into the Church, as a baby, child, or adult, is marked by baptism; growing to conscious faith as a young person or adult is marked by confirmation; and commitment to a partner for life is marked by marriage. Confession and the sacrament of reconciliation mark the restoration of the sinner to a right relationship with God; ordination marks a change of life to a calling to serve God and people as a bishop, priest, or deacon; and anointing marks progress from sickness to health or, in a final illness, from this life to the next.

- The sacraments make change happen. For example, after the sacrament of marriage, a newly married couple has a different status in society from the one they had before as single people. Someone who has publicly declared his or her faith through the sacrament of baptism is seen as a new member of the Christian community.

- The meaning of *sacrament* is most fully expressed in Jesus himself. He is God (the invisible and spiritual grace) who became human flesh (the visible and outward sign).

Thinking it through

- What in your life especially speaks of God to you? It could be a place, a person, or a happening in the past; these have sacramental value.

- Many Christians say that a priest's main job is to administer the sacraments. Why do you think they say this? What do you think?

Chapter 12
BAPTISM

Holy Baptism is full initiation by water and the Holy Spirit into Christ's Body the Church. The bond which God establishes in Baptism is indissoluble.

—*The Book of Common Prayer,* p. 298

The word "baptism" comes from the Greek word meaning to dip or immerse in water. During the service of baptism the priest pours water over the person being baptized or plunges the person under it.

Baptism normally takes place at a public Sunday service to emphasize that baptism is a public declaration of faith, making the person a member of a Christian congregation and part of the worldwide Church. However, baptism on special occasions may also take place in a private service.

The priest greets the person or persons to be baptized. Those old enough to make promises on their own behalf will be accompanied by sponsors. If the person to receive baptism is a baby, the parents and godparents are welcomed and reminded of their responsibility to see that the child is brought up as a Christian.

The service provides an opportunity to express thanksgiving. "The Liturgy of the Word and the sermon are an opportunity to set the story of what God has done in Christ alongside our own story."[1] We are encouraged to see a

The baptism service often takes place around a special baptismal font.

physically enter the church through the door, they spiritually enter the Church, the body of believers in Christ, by means of baptism.

Those to be baptized—or, if they are too young, their parents and godparents—join together with the congregation in saying the baptismal convenant, which shows that they are at one with the community of believers.

Then they go alone (or are carried) to the waters of the font to be baptized. They are supported by others, but it is also a very personal and individual experience, just like each person's birth and death. The priest immerses or pours water upon the candidate, saying "I baptize you in the Name of the Father, and of the Son, and of the Holy Spirit."

A new life has begun, one steeped in the grace of God. As a sign of this, those who have been baptized may be clothed in special white clothes (symbolizing purification) and anointed with oil as a sign of being "sealed by the Holy Spirit in Baptism and marked as Christ's own forever."

They are then commissioned to live out the baptized life and (if they are old enough) to take part in the prayers and actions of the Church.

Finally, to emphasize that the baptized have a life that takes place in worship and in the world, at the end of the service they are given a lighted candle to show that they have a mission to take Christ's light out into the world. This is lit from the Easter (Paschal) candle, which is a symbol of Christ's resurrection and victory over evil and death.

connection between the story of Christ and our own experience.

This leads to the presentation of those to be baptized and their welcome by the congregation. Together they (or, in the case of the very young, the parents and godparents on their behalf) accept their shared responsibility for seeing that the child "is brought up in the Christian faith and life" and through prayers and witness, "help this child to grow into the full stature of Christ?" This in turn leads to a renunciation [rejection] of "Satan and all the spiritual forces of wickedness that rebel against God."[2]

The action then moves to the font. This is a large basin often found close to the entrance of the church. Just as people

The meaning of baptism

Jesus began his preaching and healing ministry by being baptized in the Jordan River. The vast majority of his followers over the two-thousand years since then

Candles symbolize the newly baptized's role in taking the light of Christ out into the world.

The Decision

A large candle may be lit. The presider addresses the candidates directly, or through their parents, godparents, and sponsors

Do you renounce Satan and all the spiritual forces of wickedness that rebel against God?
I renounce them.

Do you renounce the evil powers of this world which corrupt and destroy the creatures of God?
I renounce them.

Do you renounce all sinful desires that draw you from the love of God?
I renounce them.

Do you turn to Jesus Christ and accept him as your Savior?
I do.

Do you put your whole trust in his grace and love?
I do.

Do you promise to follow and obey him as your Lord?
I do.[3]

have begun their Christian lives with baptism.

In the Episcopal Church, many people are baptized when they are babies. However, when people convert to Christianity as adults they can receive adult baptism. It is a once-and-for-all sacrament—it cannot be redone or undone.

There are several ways to understand baptism.

An act of cleansing

Have you ever stood under a waterfall? Even standing under a very powerful shower can make you feel as though your breath is being taken away. Water is a powerful symbol to show how Christ washes away a person's sins and gives a fresh start.

There is a saying that when people want to make a fresh start at something (for example, they decide to stop swearing) they are "turning over a new leaf." Christians believe that baptism is a sign that a person has decided to start living a completely new life for God. It marks the beginning of the Christian journey through life.

An act of identity

Many people wear uniforms. Some schools require them; people who work in retail often wear them, as do the police, nurses, and those serving in the armed forces. Uniforms are a way of identifying yourself with an organization or indicating what kind of work you do. However, an act of identity is not always a matter of the clothes you wear. Sometimes it involves the things you do.

A Christian is someone who identifies with Jesus Christ. The way in which Christians do this may vary from person to person (for example, some people wear a cross around their neck). However, there is one act of identity that is common to almost all Christians. It is baptism. Saint Paul describes the baptized as being "clothed...with Christ" (Galatians 3:27). The language symbolizes the stripping off at baptism of the clothes of sin (old habits) and putting on new clothes of Christ: "you have stripped off the old self with its practices and have clothed yourselves with the new self" (Colossians 3:9-10).

An act of belonging

Think of the organizations or social media networks that you are a member of or would like to join. What entrance requirements do you need to fulfil in order to belong to them? Why do they have entrance requirements?

Bravery of baptism

To your parents, if you were baptized as a baby or small child, your baptism probably seemed a very natural way of thanking God for your birth and asking God for protection and help while you were growing up.

But we need to be aware that baptism is a very brave step to take in some parts of the world: the Christian missionary organization Open Doors United Kingdom estimates that 215 million Christians face high levels of persecution today. North Korea is the most dangerous place to practice the Christian faith, followed by Afghanistan, Somalia, and Sudan. The study revealed that every month, 255 Christians are killed for their faith, 104 are abducted, and 180 Christian women are raped, sexually harassed, or forced into marriage.[4]

Baptism is an outward sign that a person belongs to the organization of God's Church. During the service the person being baptized is welcomed by the rest of the Church with the following words: "We receive you into the household of God. Confess the faith of Christ crucified, proclaim his resurrection, and share with us in his eternal priesthood."[5]

An initiation ceremony

Baptism is also a new beginning. It marks the beginning of your membership of the Church.

Baptism means being united to the death and resurrection of Jesus. It means we are asked to "die" to our old, sinful self and grow up as a new person in the light of Christ. It is also a promise that when we die, we will share the eternal life of Jesus.

In the Episcopal Church, when babies are baptized they become part of the family of God's Church. Augustine, one of the Church Fathers, compared what happens at baptism to the mark or seal that in Augustine's day was tattooed on a soldier to show who was his lord and master. Baptism is a mark that God is the lord of the child's life. When adults convert to Christianity in their baptism they promise to turn around from their old way of life and to follow Christ.

Another name for baptism is *christening*. This is sometimes called *Christianing*—being made a Christian. The person receives the Holy Spirit into his or her life. Frequently, anointing with *chrism* (oil mixed with fragrant spices) is used as a sign of the blessings brought by the Holy Spirit. At the anointing, a cross or the ancient *Chi-Rho* sign (which consists of the first two letters in Greek of the name

"Christ," i.e. "Anointed one") may be made on the forehead of the person who has been baptized.

A death and a resurrection

In the early days of Christianity, baptism was normally intended for adults and was performed at Easter time. Jesus called his death and resurrection a baptism. To his apostles he said: "Are you able to drink the cup that I drink, or be baptized with the baptism that I am baptized with?" (Mark 10:38). Saint Paul used the image of dying and rising to new life to explain the meaning of baptism:

> We who died to sin…we have been buried with [Jesus] by baptism into death, so that, just as Christ was raised from the dead by the glory of the Father, so we too might walk in newness of life. We know that our old self was crucified with him so that the body of sin might be destroyed, and we might no longer be enslaved to sin.
> Romans 6:2-6

Paul means that all our lives long we are struggling to leave behind our old, natural life of sin and selfishness, to try and grow more like Christ. He also sees baptism as a guarantee that when this life is over, we will share with Christ in eternal life.

> I did not get baptized as a baby, but when I was 21. I wanted to make a new beginning and let Jesus rule my life from now on.
> Carrie

At baptism the child receives the gift of the Holy Spirit. From earliest times the

Sometimes baptism is called a *christening* or a *Christianing*. What do you think about those names?

giving of the Holy Spirit has been associated with baptism (Acts 8:14-17).

It is the Holy Spirit that leads us to grow in faith as we journey on our pilgrimage through life. This is reflected in the following prayer from the baptism service:

Heavenly Father, we thank you that by water and the Holy Spirit you have bestowed upon these your servants the forgiveness of sin, and have raised them to the new life of grace.

Sustain them, O Lord, in your Holy Spirit. Give them an inquiring and discerning heart, the courage to will and to persevere, a spirit to know and to love you, and the gift of joy and wonder in all your works. Amen.[6]

Today most Episcopalians are baptized by "sprinkling" of water. Some prefer a full dunking. Either way is fine. What really matters is the act of baptism, not the amount of water used!

The Baptismal Promises

An important part of the Baptismal Convenant are five promises. These promises are central to the life and faith of Episcopalians. The promises are in the form of questions, with the answer to each being, "I will, with God's help."

- Will you continue in the apostles' teaching and fellowship, in the breaking, and in the prayers?

- Will you persevere in resisting evil, and, whenever you fall into sin, repent and return to the Lord?

- Will you proclaim by word and example the Good News of God in Christ?

- Will you seek and serve Christ in all persons, loving your neighbor as yourself?

- Will you strive for justice and peace among all people, and respect the dignity of every human being?[7]

- Prayers follow the baptismal promises, with the congregation beseeching, "Lord, hear our prayer." At the end of the prayer, the celebrant says, "Grant, O Lord, that all who are baptized into the death of Jesus Christ your Son may live in the power of his resurrection and look for him to come again in glory; who lives and reigns now and for ever. Amen."[7]

Thinking it through

- Why do you think that baptisms usually take place today in the presence of the congregation at the main Sunday service? Why is baptism so important?

- What is the symbolic meaning of the following in the baptism service: pouring water over the person's head; making the sign of the cross on the person's head; anointing with chrism; giving the person a lighted candle? Why is the candle lit from the Easter (Paschal) candle?

- Often parents ask for baptism for their baby because they think it is a nice celebration or because the grandparents want it. Do you think these are good enough reasons? Do you think the Church should baptize children of parents who are not Christians?

Bible Study

Read the story of Jesus' baptism at the beginning of Matthew's Gospel (Matthew 3:13-17).

Jesus goes down to the Jordan River where he is baptized by John the Baptist. The Holy Spirit descends upon him and a voice comes from heaven declaring that Jesus is God's beloved Son.

- Why was John the Baptist reluctant to baptize Jesus?

- What does the voice of God tell us about Jesus' importance?

- Why do you think that Jesus was tempted by the devil immediately after his baptism?

FOR PRAYER & REFLECTION

Almighty and everliving God,
let your fatherly hand ever be
over these your servants;
let your Holy Spirit ever be with them;
and so lead them in the knowledge
and obedience of your Word,
that they may serve you in this life,
and dwell with you in the life to come;
through Jesus Christ our Lord.
Amen.[8]

Some prayer **topics**

For help in turning to Christ.

To be able to repent of our sins each day.

To fight against evil in our lives and in the world.

Chapter 13

CONFIRMATION

In the course of their Christian development, those baptized at an early age are expected, when they are ready and have been duly prepared, to make a mature public affirmation of their faith and commitment to the responsibilities of their Baptism and to receive the laying on of hands by the bishop.

—*The Book of Common Prayer,* p. 412

Standing up for what you believe

As children we often adopt the beliefs, opinions, and ideas of our parents. However, during adolescence we start to develop our own more distinct personalities and individual tastes, beliefs, and values. For some of us, this is a turbulent time, when we find ourselves rebelling against our parents and other authority figures. For others, the changes in personality and lifestyle come relatively peacefully. We have more choice in what we wear; the music, films, and books we like; the places where we go; our subject choices at school; and what we plan to do when we leave school.

This transition from childhood to adulthood is often characterized by a determination to stand up for what we believe. Also society grants us more freedoms: We can go out on our own and stay out later; when we are 16 we can learn to drive a car, and when we're 18 we can vote. But with greater freedom comes greater responsibility.

Within Christianity this transition to taking adult responsibility is marked by the sacrament of confirmation. It is a time when young people confirm for themselves the promises that their parents and godparents may have made for them at their baptism, or perhaps when they make those promises for themselves, being both baptized and confirmed at the same time.

Confirmation involves taking responsibility for your religious faith. It is a time when you yourself publicly declare that you want to belong to the Church. You do this by making a profession (formal statement) of faith before a bishop, who serves as a representative of the universal Church. It is also a time when people receive the gifts of the Holy Spirit in a special way.

However, confirmation is not just for teenagers. Many adults become confirmed later on in their life—they may have been baptized as babies but they did not grow up in the Christian faith. Later they come back to the Church and want to make a public affirmation of their faith.

Taking a stand can be costly

In some communist countries, Christians are persecuted and face imprisonment if they don't renounce their beliefs:

> *An abducted and detained Degar Christian villager named Y-Huong Nie was given a five-year prison term for refusing to sign a document renouncing his religious beliefs on 4 July, 2011. Y-Huong Nie was abducted by security police on September 15, 2010 and has been in prison in Dak Lak province ever since.*
>
> from a newsletter supporting Degar Christians in Vietnam[1]

Although being a Christian in the United States does not bring such punishments, it can still carry a cost.

> *Sometimes I find it difficult standing up for what I believe. It can make me unpopular with my friends, especially when they want to do something that I disagree with. They start to say that I am no fun. It would be so much easier sometimes to follow the crowd.*
>
> James

The origins of confirmation

In the early Church, baptism and the "laying on of hands" were performed on adult converts (Acts 8:17; 19:6). However, the two acts of baptism and laying on of hands became separate in the Western Church as baptism began to be carried out at the Easter Vigil in parishes where the bishop was not present. The laying on of hands by the bishop then had to wait until it could be performed later in the sacrament of confirmation.

The meaning of confirmation

Confirmation continues what was begun at baptism and celebrates the presence and work of the Holy Spirit within us. It also marks full membership of the Church.

Being an ambassador

Ambassadors are meant to represent the beliefs, values, culture, and interests of their countries abroad.

When Christians are confirmed, they reaffirm the promises that were made for them at baptism (or, if they are baptized and confirmed at the same time, they

Traditionally, confirmands kneel before a bishop, who places hands on the head and confirms the person, saying these words: "Strengthen, O Lord, your servant, with your Holy Spirit; empower him for your service and sustain him all the days of his life. *Amen.*"

What happens at a confirmation service?

*   The confirmation service is led by a bishop, who represents the universal Church. This emphasizes the importance of confirmation. It starts with the people being confirmed renewing their baptismal promises— which were made on their behalf by their parents and godparents if they were baptized as infants—and agreeing to take responsibility for them.

*   The confirmation candidates make a profession of faith. They do this by joining with the congregation in saying the Apostles' Creed and the baptismal promises.

*   The bishop asks the Holy Spirit to come and rest upon the confirmation candidates. At the heart of this sacrament, as of all sacraments, is the giving of God's power, the Holy Spirit. The bishop's hands are stretched out toward the confirmation candidates, and the bishop prays that they will be given the gifts of the Holy Spirit.

*   The bishop addresses each candidate by name, saying, "Strengthen, O Lord, your servant, with your Holy Spirit; empower him for your service; and sustain him all the days of his life. *Amen*" or "Defend, O Lord, your servant N. with your heavenly grace, that she may continue yours for ever, and daily increase in your Holy Spirit more and more, until she comes to your everlasting kingdom. *Amen.*"[2]

make the promises on their own behalf). They take upon themselves the responsibility to represent Christ in the world. They are Christ's ambassadors— God's co-workers in the world.

How is a candidate prepared for confirmation?

To prepare the candidates for confirmation the priest will hold classes to instruct them as to what it means to accept the Christian faith and to live as a Christian in the world. Confirmation classes might last for a few months or sometimes longer.

- The bishop then makes the sign of a cross on the candidate's foreheads, using chrism oil. The bishop concludes with a prayer, beseeching God to "let your Holy Spirit ever be with them; and so lead them in the knowledge and obedience of your Word."[3] The laying on of hands by the bishop reflects the custom of the apostles, who laid on hands when they prayed for someone to receive special gifts (Acts 13:1-3).

- Chrism—oil mixed with fragrant spices—may accompany confirmation. This expresses the richness of the Holy Spirit. The word *chrism*, like *Christ*, comes from the Greek word meaning "to anoint." From Old Testament times, prophets, priests, and kings have been anointed with oil as a sign of the Spirit empowering them to fulfil their special calling. Accompanied by the sign of the cross, God anoints the candidates with the Spirit, to enable them to fulfil the special work he wants them to do in their Christian lives

- The newly confirmed candidates share the peace and then partake in Holy Eucharist.

Bishops lay hands on the confirmand as a reminder of how the apostles laid hands on people when they prayed for them to receive special gifts.

Family and friends celebrate confirmation as an important step in the journey of faith. Who will you invite to celebrate with you?

Thinking it through

- Have you ever had to stand up for what you believe in? Have you ever found yourself in a situation in which following God looks like the most difficult way?

- What do you think is meant by the promise a confirmation candidate makes to reject all that is evil? Make a list of things you may need to reject. Think about which area of your life is most difficult to give totally to God.

- Do you think there is an ideal age at which to be confirmed?

Bible Study

Read Galatians 5:16-25. This is one of the suggested readings for the confirmation service.

- Paul starts by describing a battle going on within the person. Inside us there is a pull to do what we know is wrong. We are often disappointed because our best efforts are not enough to make us better than we are. Try to provide examples of what Paul might be referring to when he talks about "the flesh" and "what the Spirit desires" (verses 16-18).

- According to Paul what sort of behavior is to be avoided as you grow in the Christian life (verses 19-21)? Why do you think these things are to be avoided?

- In this passage Paul goes on to describe the marks of a Christian life which are produced by the Holy Spirit working in you. What qualities does he refer to (verses 22-25)?

FOR PRAYER & REFLECTION

Sometimes, the bishop presides over receptions and reaffirmations. A reception is typically someone who is from another Christian tradition and may already have been confirmed but would like to be received into the Episcopal Church. A reaffirmation may be for someone who has been away from the church for a long time but would like to reaffirm a commitment. The bishop says these prayers:

For Reception

> *We recognize you as a member of the one holy catholic and apostolic Church, and we receive you into the fellowship of this Communion. God, the Father, Son, and Holy Spirit, bless, preserve, and keep you. Amen.*

For Reaffirmation

> *May the Holy Spirit, who has begun a good work in you, direct and uphold you in the service of Christ and his kingdom. Amen.*[4]

Some prayer **topics**

For inward strength to stand up for your beliefs.

For guidance in understanding God's will for your life.

For help in living the Christian life, and showing forth the qualities of the Holy Spirit within you.

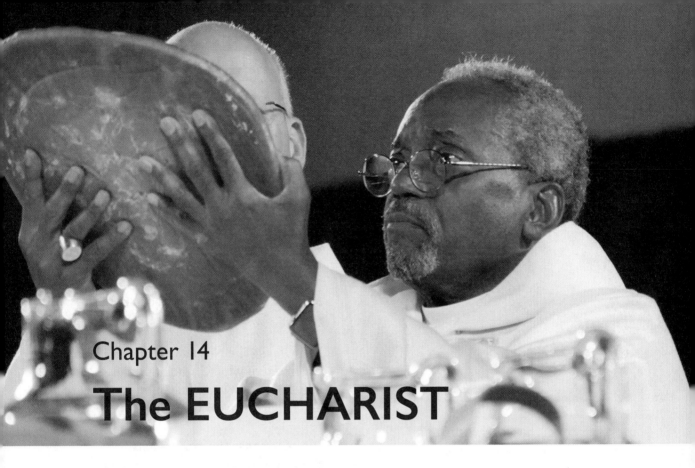

Chapter 14
The EUCHARIST

The Gifts of God for the People of God.
Take them in remembrance that Christ died for you,
and feed on him in your hearts by faith,
with thanksgiving.

—*The Book of Common Prayer*, p. 364-65

A grandmother in her late seventies wears several rings on her left hand, including a simple gold one that is very old. It belonged to her mother and before that to her mother's mother. She has worn it for thirty years, as did her mother. It is the only really personal thing of her mother's that she has. While it is indistinguishable from dozens of other gold rings, for her it is irreplaceable as it helps to keep the memory of her mother alive.

For Christians, the eucharist is precious and irreplaceable. It gives us a unique way of being close to Jesus.

What happens at the eucharist?

The style of services varies considerably. Some are grand services, and others very simple—imagine an army chaplain giving communion to soldiers living in tents or a priest offering the eucharist during a service for people who are living on the streets. Some services will have a lot of ritual (bells, incense, etc.) and others very little. Some will use communion wafers, others a simple loaf of bread. In

Holy Eucharist is the primary service for most Episcopal churches on Sunday mornings.

Collect: There are special prayers for each week in the Church's calendar and for saints' days. These are intended to introduce the readings.

Bible readings: From both the Old and the New Testaments, concluding with a Gospel reading, for which all stand. There may be three, two, or—rarely—only one reading, but there is always a reading from one of the gospels.

Sermon: To explain and teach about the readings and apply them to people's lives.

The Creed: The Nicene Creed, a statement of what Christians believe, may be said by everyone but it is not used at every service.

Intercessions: The prayers and thanksgiving of the people are offered. These may follow a set form or be written for the particular service.

Penitence: In preparation to hear God's Word, the people confess their sins and receive absolution.

most Episcopal churches, vestments (ceremonial clothes) will be worn, while in some situations, the clergy may wear their ordinary clothes.

The Episcopal Church offers forms of service for the celebration of the eucharist in modern language and more traditional. These forms of service fall into two main parts: the Liturgy of the Word and the Liturgy of the Table. Within those are several different components.

Liturgy of the Word

Here, a breakdown of a typical eucharistic service is given.

Greeting: Having gathered together, the people are greeted by the priest.

Kyrie eleison and Gloria: These will be used according to the season of the Church's year (e.g. the Gloria is not sung in Lent); they are not generally used when the eucharist is celebrated on a weekday.

Sometimes the eucharist is celebrated in formal services. At other times, it can take place within an informal service. This eucharist is part of an active faith initiative at St. Matthew's Episcopal Church in Austin, Texas.

The Peace: A handshake or embrace is exchanged to remind us that Christians make up one body united in mutual love.

Liturgy of the Table

The Eucharistic Prayer: The presider (bishop or priest), in dialogue with the people, recalls God's saving acts, gives thanks over the bread and wine and says the words that Jesus himself said at the Last Supper. The bread and wine are consecrated in this prayer. Some presiders show their reverence for the moment of consecration and the presence of Christ in the sacrament by one or more of the following actions: bending the right knee (genuflecting); censing (using incense); elevating the bread and wine (lifting them up for people to see); and/or ringing bells.

The bread is broken (the fraction): After the bread has been broken, the presider invites the people to receive the Body and Blood of Christ.

At communion, the priest or other minister places a wafer or piece of bread in the hand of the communicant, saying, "The Body of Christ" or similar words.

In many churches, after the service some of the consecrated bread is placed in a safe called an aumbry or tabernacle, so that it is readily available to be taken to

Christian beliefs about the eucharist

- The eucharist is the most important act of worship for many Christians. Episcopalians and Anglicans all over the world, like the great majority of Christians, gather and repeat an action that Jesus performed with his disciples on the night before he died. Kings and queens take part in it after they have been crowned; married couples celebrate it after their wedding; and the dying receive it on their deathbed.

- Jesus celebrated a last supper with his disciples on the night before he died. Ever since then, Christians have obeyed Jesus' command to repeat his actions. The Acts of the Apostles tells us how the early Christians met regularly for the "breaking of bread" (Acts 2:42). In the eucharist we often say or sing the canticle, "Lamb of God, you take away the sins of the world." This reminds us that at the Last Supper, Jesus put himself in the place of the Passover Lamb, and that the eucharist is our new, Christian Passover meal.

- The eucharist unites us to Christ's sacrifice on the cross. As we receive the sacrament, we not only remember Jesus' self-offering, but also we are united with it, and a freely given gift (grace) becomes effective in our lives. Jesus' sacrifice was costly; it shows us how much God loves us, enough to send his only Son to die for us.

- We human beings are not creatures of spirit only: We are also made of flesh and blood. That's why Jesus himself became incarnate to save us. In a way, Jesus is incarnate in the eucharist again. He comes not only spiritually but also physically as the consecrated bread and wine. Like all the sacraments, the eucharist is more than words. Even in an ordinary relationship, a single hug can sometimes mean more than many words. In the eucharist, Jesus gives us this physical expression of his love to express and sustain our relationship with him.

sick people who cannot come to church. A white light burns near the place where the sacrament is reserved, usually in a side chapel where people can go for private prayer. Many find such a quiet place very helpful and may genuflect as a sign of reverence.

Sending Out: At the end of the service the people, having heard God's Word and having been nourished by Christ's body and blood, go out to be witnesses of Christ in the world and to continue Christ's work. The priest blesses them and dismisses them.

Some facts about the eucharist

- **The word eucharist means thanksgiving**: Jesus "gave thanks" over the bread and wine. When Christians repeat this command they are:

  giving thanks, as Jesus did, for all the good things of nature (represented by the bread and wine);

  calling to mind what Jesus was about to do (die on the cross) and giving thanks for Jesus' offering;

  asking God to make Jesus present again.

- **The eucharist involves the fourfold action: taking, giving thanks, breaking, and sharing**. At the eucharist, the presider (a bishop or priest who presides over the sacrament) repeats Jesus' actions. Everyone gathers around the altar to re-enact the meal Jesus had with his disciples. The presider takes the bread and wine, says a prayer over them, breaks the bread, and shares the elements. However much the language or ceremony vary, all eucharists contain these actions.

- **Debate about the meaning of the eucharist has been one of the main points of division between the denominations**. However, after centuries of argument about what Jesus meant by giving us his body and blood, there are some encouraging signs of agreement. Our focus is on the real, objective presence of Jesus in the consecrated bread and wine. Put simply, in some way we do not fully understand, Jesus really gives himself to us in the community sharing the consecrated bread and wine. The bread and wine are really changed (that is why they must either be consumed or carefully reserved after the service), and they become the means of his being present with us and in us.

- **This sacrament is known by a number of names**. Apart from *eucharist*, some Christians refer to it as *Holy Communion*, which draws attention to the belief that Christians meet Christ in the bread and wine and that this celebration takes place in the company of all Christians, and with angels and archangels, and with all the company of heaven. Some call it the *Last Supper*, recalling Jesus' meal with his disciples. Other Christians call it the *Mass*, which comes from the closing words of the service in its Latin form (*Ite, missa est*—"Go, you are sent out into the world"). Regardless of what we call the eucharist, we are strengthened by the meal that we have shared and sent into the world to "'go in peace to love and serve the Lord."

The meaning of the eucharist

Since the eucharist is very important and precious to Christians, it is important too that we prepare ourselves thoroughly for it. Saint Paul warns against eating the Lord's Supper without proper preparation (1 Corinthians 11:27-29): We must approach it with the right attitude. We should take going to each eucharist seriously, which is one of the reasons why the service includes the confession of sins and asking for God's forgiveness.

The following story shows the importance of the right attitude:

One day the Emperor Napoleon with one of his servants decided to go out into the town disguised as ordinary citizens. They went to an inn for a meal. At the end of the meal the landlady brought them a bill for 14 francs. They searched in their

During the eucharistic prayer, the bread and wine are blessed and consecrated. They are sometimes lifted up and shown to the congregation to emphasize what has happened and to encourage a prayerful response.

At communion, the priest or other minister places a wafer or piece of bread in the hand of the communicant, saying, "The body of Christ" or similar words.

pockets for money but to their embarrassment found none. They promised to bring back the money within the hour.

The landlady would not hear of it. She threatened to fetch the police if she was not paid at once. The waiter felt sorry for the two gentlemen and offered to pay the bill for them—"they seem honest men." So they were able to leave the inn without the police being called.

How do you feel when you receive the communion wafer or bread? What is your most significant experience of receiving the eucharist?

Within hours the servant returned to the inn and asked the landlady how much she had bought it for. She replied, 30,000 francs, at which point the servant handed the landlady the money for the inn and told her: "On the emperor's orders I am commanded to present this inn to the waiter who helped him out in his need."
Pierre Lefèvre, *One Hundred Stories to Change Your Life*[1]

The landlady and the waiter reacted very differently to the same two men. As a result the landlady lost her inn and the waiter received a rich reward. Christians believe that when they receive Jesus' body

and blood in the form of bread and wine, it is important that they have the right attitude.

When they have the right attitude, Christians find receiving communion a powerful experience:

> *Every time I've received communion it feels like a fresh start—I can go out into the world trying to love others all over again.*
> Kwamie, 17

> *It is my spiritual food—it gives me strength for all that I have to do in the day.*
> Kimberly, 24

> *The eucharist is important to me because I feel that it brings me closer to my brother who died two years ago. It is a spiritual meal in which we join together with all Christians and the heavenly host.*
> James, 18

We come together in the Body of Christ. We share Holy Communion and are then sent out to carry on the work of Jesus. As Saint Augustine put it: "You are the Body of Christ: You are to be taken, consecrated, broken, and distributed, that you may be the means of grace" to others.

The gifts of God, for the people of God.

Thinking it through

- How do you think you should prepare for receiving communion?

- Why do you think the eucharist is so important to many Christians?

- Some countries do not grow grapes and do not have the raw materials to make bread. What alternatives could Christians use to celebrate the eucharist?

Bible Study

Read the account of the Last Supper in Luke 22:14-23.

On the night before he died Jesus shared a last meal with his closest disciples. The Eucharist is based upon this last supper. During the meal Jesus says a special prayer over the bread and the wine.

- What conversation did Jesus have with his disciples during the meal? How did the disciples react to what Jesus said?

- Bread and wine were normal everyday foods. What special meaning did Jesus give to the bread and to the wine?

- The bread was broken. What does this breaking point to? The wine was poured. What does this pouring refer to?

FOR PRAYER & REFLECTION

Almighty and everliving God,
we thank you for feeding us with the
spiritual food of the most precious
Body and Blood of your Son our Savior
Jesus Christ;
and for assuring us in these holy mysteries
that we are living members of the Body of
your Son, and heirs of your eternal
kingdom.
And now, Father, send us out
to do the work you have given us to do,
to love and serve you as faithful witnesses
of Christ our Lord.
To him, to you, and to the Holy Spirit,
be honor and glory, now and for ever.
Amen.[2]

Some prayer **topics**

Ask God to make our hearts pure so that we can come to celebrate the eucharist.

Ask God to forgive us our sins—to give us a new start.

Thank Jesus for his willingness to have his body broken on the cross and his blood poured out—for showing his love for us.

Ask God that through the eucharist he will give us his spiritual food—to strengthen us in our faith by the Holy Spirit.

Chapter 15

MARRIAGE

The bond and covenant of marriage was established by God in creation, and our Lord Jesus Christ adorned this manner of life by his presence and first miracle at a wedding in Cana of Galilee. It signifies to us the mystery of the union between Christ and his Church, and Holy Scripture commends it to be honored among all people.

—*The Book of Common Prayer*, p. 423

What do you think about marriage? Can you see yourself getting married? Given that a growing number of people simply live together, why do you think some people decide to take marriage vows? What is special about being married?

Fifty or so years ago most people got married in church. But some people are deciding against marriage. Are there good reasons for getting married or do you think that marriage is out of date?

What does the Church say about marriage? What do you think?

What happens at a wedding service?

- The priest welcomes everybody present and reminds them of the reasons for marriage.

- Bible passages (usually on the theme of love and marriage) are read and a homily is preached.

A church wedding doesn't necessarily have to be in church. The sacrament of marriage may be shared in different places, including outdoors.

- The two people declare their intention to marry and the congregation is asked if they will support them.

- The two exchange vows with each other: "to have and to hold from this day forward; for better for worse, for richer for poorer, in sickness and in health, to love and to cherish, until we are parted by death."[1]

- Wedding rings are blessed and exchanged as a sign of the vows that have just been taken. The ring symbolizes the everlasting love between the two people.

- The priest blesses the married couple.

- Prayers are offered for the couple.

The wedding ceremony is sometimes followed by a celebration of the eucharist.

Declaration of Intention

According to the canons of the Episcopal Church, all those seeking marriage in the Episcopal Church must sign the following Declaration of Intention: "We understand the teaching of the church that God's purpose for our marriage is for our mutual joy; for the help and comfort we will give to each other in prosperity and adversity; and, when it is God's will, for the gift and heritage of children and their nurture in the knowledge and love of God. We also understand that our marriage is to be unconditional, mutual, exclusive, faithful, and lifelong; and we engage to make the utmost effort to accept these gifts and fulfill these duties, with the help of God and the support of our community."

Christian beliefs about marriage

• **Married love was created by God.** It is part of God's plan for humanity and as such is sacred. In the story of the creation of the world God created Eve and then the man said: "'This at last is bone of my bones and flesh of my flesh'... Therefore a man leaves his father and his mother and clings to his wife, and they become one flesh" (Genesis 2:23,24).

• **Marriage is for life.** First, this is to enable people to feel secure in their love. It is also important that children brought up in a family feel secure. Second, a lifetime commitment in marriage gives two people the space to learn to love in an unselfish way; as they do this, they reflect God's love. The hallmarks of a married relationship are loyalty and faithfulness, but sometimes marriages break down (see the "Some facts about marriage" box on the next page).

• **Marriage is protected.** Because marriage is created by God and is part of God's plan for people, it is protected in the Bible by a commandment: "You shall not commit adultery" (Exodus 20:14; Deuteronomy 5:18).

• **Marriage is the proper context for sexual intercourse.** The Bible says that when two people have sex they become "one flesh" and for this reason Christians believe that the correct place for sex is within the relationship of complete commitment that marriage provides. In sex two people become one in a very real way —yes, physically, but also emotionally and spiritually; they become completely open with each other and share their greatest intimacy. However, many couples who ask for a church wedding are already living together, and many priests, while they don't condone this, focus on the couple's desire to enter into the full commitment of marriage.

• **Marriage is blessed by God.** God is the third partner in Christian marriage. The love that two people share in Christian marriage is a sign of God's love. When two people promise unconditional love to each other for life, they show what Christ's own sacrificial love is like.

The wedding registers are signed either after the blessing of the couple or at the end of the service.

Marriage is about selfless love

Being able to love and care for the other person in a selfless way is the sign of a good and mature marriage. It is a mirror of God's selfless love for us.

When I'm preaching at weddings, I often tell the wedding congregation about couples in the parish who have been married for a long time. Far from being restrictive, marriage seems to have helped them grow as individuals. In an unselfish way, they have learned to compensate for each other's weaknesses and admire each other's strengths. And a sign of how far this selfless love goes is the way I've so often seen one spouse caring so lovingly for the other when they're afflicted by the illnesses of old age.

A parish priest

Some facts about marriage

- Marriage is a public announcement. It is important to make these vows publicly—they bind a couple in front of witnesses and before God.

- Sometimes marriages break down beyond repair. When this happens, the Church offers pastoral support. Generally, a divorced person may have a second marriage in church. However, this is at the discretion of the parish priest and, normally, the bishop's permission must also be given. Otherwise, a couple may have a civil ceremony, followed by a service of prayer and dedication.

- The variety of practice about remarriage in church reflects a spectrum of sincerely held belief. Some Christians point to Jesus' teaching in Mark 10:2-12, which forbids divorce (a break with the custom of his day, which allowed a man to divorce and remarry). Others point to Matthew 5:31-32, where Jesus permits divorce on grounds of adultery. This, they argue, implies that Jesus foresaw that there might be a need for exceptions. They also point to his general teaching about the need for forgiveness. On this basis, they argue that the Church should be forgiving toward those whose marriages have failed and give them a second chance. Some also refer to the practice of Orthodox Christians who regard a failed marriage as dead and permit an additional one, as long as the couple is penitent about the earlier failure.

The rings are outward signs of the couple's promises. Wedding rings have no end and are a symbol of permanence.

"Until we are parted by death"

Marriage is a lifelong commitment, as the following story illustrates:

> Duke Wasa of Poland was imprisoned on a charge of treason and his wife, Katherina Jagello, asked the king of Sweden to allow her to share her husband's imprisonment. The king resisted her request, reminding her that her husband's sentence was for life and that he would never enjoy the status of a duke again. She told the king that she understood this but that nevertheless the duke was her husband, to which the king replied that she could leave him and marry someone else. However, Katherina showed the king her wedding ring and asked him to read the words inscribed on it—Mors sola—"Death alone can part us." Katherina ultimately shared seventeen years of imprisonment with her husband and she was only released after the king's death.
>
> Pierre Lefèvre, *One Hundred Stories to Change Your Life*[2]

Marriage inclusivity

The issue of whether marriage may only be between a man and a woman has been settled within the Episcopal Church. While the issue has been controversial for some, the General Convention has proclaimed the Episcopal Church as a welcoming and affirming place for all people, regardless of sexual orientation. Acts of General Convention have opened the sacramental rite of marriage to same-sex couples in the Episcopal Church. Already, same-sex couples have equal rights to civil marriage throughout the United States, after a June 26, 2015 ruling by the U.S. Supreme Court.

The resolutions passed by General Convention are clear: the normative teaching of the church is that same-sex marriage is legal and covenantal. At the same time, the decision was not unanimous, and some Episcopalians do not support same-sex marriage. To accommodate the wide and deeply held views on this issue, the Episcopal Church has made provisions for those who disagree with offering the rite of marriage to same-sex couples.

Currently, *The Book of Common Prayer's* liturgy still includes gendered references and refers to marriage as "between a man and a woman." For the moment, the Episcopal Church has two distinct sets of liturgies: the Celebration and Blessing of a Marriage in *The Book of Common Prayer* and the liturgies that are authorized for trial use. This is, in part, because it takes two successive General Conventions (a total of six years) to change text in *The Book of Common Prayer*. It is likely that process will begin soon, but it has not happened yet.[3]

During the marriage service, the union is blessed by God.
The love that two people share in Christian marriage is a sign of God's love.

Thinking it through

- Many people today live together instead of getting married. Why do you think they do this? What do you think are the advantages of

    (a) living together,

    (b) getting married?

    What does Christian teaching say about this?

- What difference does it make to get married in church? If you marry, where would you like the ceremony to take place and why?

- What do you think about the Church's traditional teaching about not marrying divorced people? Do you think that allowing the priest the discretion to permit remarriage is a good thing?

- How do you think the Church should carry out Jesus' teaching in the following situations?

    (a) When a young unmarried couple ask the parish priest for their baby to be baptized;

    (b) When an unmarried couple discover that they are expecting a child.

Bible Study

Read Paul's advice on marriage in his letter to the Ephesians (Ephesians 5:21-33).

According to this passage:

- What is the proper relationship between two people in marriage?

- In what ways does Paul compare the marriage relationship with Christ's relationship to the Church?

- What do you think it means for two people to become one body?

FOR PRAYER & REFLECTION

O God, you have so consecrated the covenant of marriage that in it is represented the spiritual unity between Christ and his Church:
Send therefore your blessing upon these your servants, that they may so love, honor, and cherish each other
in faithfulness and patience, in wisdom and true godliness, that their home may be a haven of blessing and peace;
through Jesus Christ our Lord, who lives and reigns with you and the Holy Spirit, one God, now and for ever. Amen.[4]

Some prayer **topics**

Ask God's help in our own personal relationships.

For God to protect our families from harm.

Help for people having problems in their relationships.

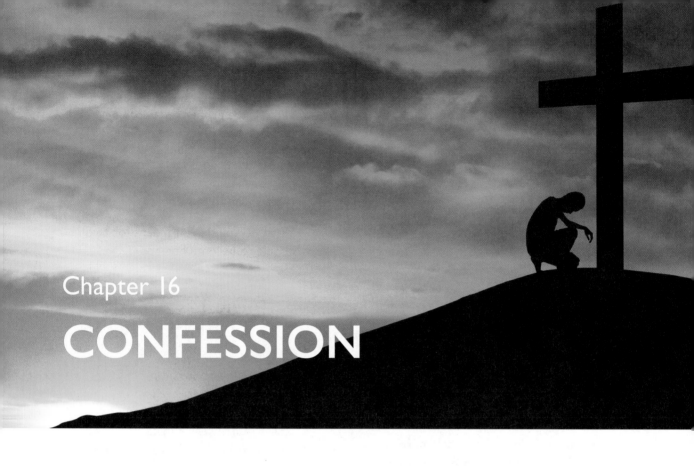

Chapter 16
CONFESSION

Almighty God, to you all hearts are open, all desires known, and from you no secrets are hid: Cleanse the thoughts of our hearts by the inspiration of your Holy Spirit, that we may perfectly love you, and worthily magnify your holy Name; through Christ our Lord. Amen.

—*The Book of Common Prayer*, p. 355

At the beginning of the eucharist, we use this prayer, The Collect for Purity, to ask God to cleanse our minds so that we are prepared to receive communion.

Saying sorry

- What sort of things do you have arguments with your friends about?

- How do you make peace after you have had a fight? Do you always wait

for the other person to say sorry or do you take the first step?

Every day we hear story after story of people who are falling out with one another: celebrities splitting up; political debates; and armed conflict breaking out. It is much rarer to read stories that tell of people making peace with one another.

Imagine that you are at a friend's house and you break something valuable. What would you do? How do you think your friend would react? Do you find it easy to say sorry to somebody you have wronged? What makes it difficult?

Sometimes "sorry" is the hardest word to say, because none of us likes admitting we have done something wrong. It is easier to sweep it under the rug and hope that nobody finds out.

As Christians we believe that when we have done something wrong (when we sin, i.e. fall short of God's design for us), we not only hurt the person we have wronged but we also hurt God because we have turned away from God's perfect will for us. We therefore need to ask God to forgive us. One of the sacraments of the Church is the sacrament of reconciliation, otherwise known as confession. In confession we admit what we have done wrong and ask for God's forgiveness. In return God makes peace with us (i.e. is reconciled with us) and gives us a fresh start.

The priest is with us at confession to help us unload the burden of our sin to God and to pronounce God's words of forgiveness. We can use different images to describe this getting rid of the things that weigh us down: It's like turning over a new leaf or deleting the sins from the computer's hard drive.

There is no rule about how often we need to go to confession. Within the Episcopal Church, there is a great variety of practice. Some Episcopal penitents (those intending to make a confession):

*   make a regular appointment to see their priest-confessor. Apart from making their confession, they may also use the opportunity to talk about their spiritual life (believing that regular confession is as good for their spiritual health as going to the dentist regularly is for their teeth.);

Making confession need not be very formal, although it usually takes place in church.

*   go to confession when they feel the need, during a particular season (such as Lent), or when something in particular is troubling them;

*   do not formally go to confession but may have a spiritual director;

*   ask God privately to forgive them their sins.

However, you can't seek to ease your conscience through confession if you ignore your responsibility toward society:

> *If individuals...seek reconciliation and pardon in the sacrament of penance, they should be signs of reconciliation amid the conflicts of society. How could they, in all sincerity of heart, seek and find reconciliation privately in the sacrament, if in their outside lives, their work, and their business affairs, they continue to exploit their fellow human beings, to pay unjust wages.*
>
> Leonardo Boff, *Sacraments of Life, Life of the Sacraments*[1]

What happens in confession?

1 **Prepare before you go to confession.** Think carefully about how you have acted, thought, and felt. Have a clear idea about what you are going to say. This is called an examination of conscience. Some people find it helpful to write down what they want to confess.

2 **Going in.** In the Episcopal Church, confession is often done with the priest and person sitting near one another or perhaps in a side chapel with a special prayer desk where you kneel to make confession.

3 **What to say?** The way you make your confession can be informal or formal. You may be given a card with words that can help guide the confession, such as "Bless me, for I have sinned." Then you confess your sins in your own words.

4 **The priest will talk to you.** The priest is there to help you and give guidance, not to make you feel guilty or issue punishments. There is probably nothing you have said (or done) that the priest hasn't heard before. Confession is a time to ask for help in how to overcome sin and grow spiritually. The priest will then give some advice, encouragement and a penance—this usually takes the form of a prayer or reading which the priest suggests as an act of thanksgiving for forgiveness, to be repeated in your own prayers later.

Words of absolution

During the sacrament of reconciliation the priest declares Christ's forgiveness to us in a personal way.
Our Lord Jesus Christ,
who offered himself to be sacrificed for us to the Father,
and who conferred power on his Church to forgive sins,
absolve you through my ministry by the grace of the Holy Spirit,
and restore you in the perfect peace of the Church. Amen.[2]

5 **Say the act of contrition** (i.e. how sorry you are).

6 **Receive absolution.** The priest will pronounce God's forgiveness and will bless you.

The meaning of confession

Confession is often called the sacrament of penance or the sacrament of reconciliation. This describes the twofold action of this sacrament: A person says sorry to God and asks for forgiveness, and in return receives God's forgiveness and is reconciled to God again.

Confession gives us a new start

In 1994 a new multi-racial government came into power in South Africa. Until then blacks and whites had been kept separate under the apartheid system, which greatly disadvantaged black South Africans. One of the key questions was, how could relationships between white and black South Africans be mended? On December 15, 1995, the new South African president, Nelson Mandela, established the Truth and Reconciliation Commission. For two years, the commission met to hear accounts of the injustices and persecution black people had experienced. It encouraged whites to come forward to take responsibility and apologize for what they had done under apartheid. Those who confessed in this way were allowed a new start. The commission was led by Archbishop Desmond Tutu.

I hope that the work of the Commission, by opening wounds to cleanse them, will thereby stop them from festering. We cannot be facile and say bygones will be bygones, because they will . . . return to haunt us. True reconciliation is never cheap, for it is based on forgiveness which is costly. Forgiveness in turn depends on repentance, which has to be based on an acknowledgment of what was done wrong, and therefore on disclosure of the truth.
Archbishop Desmond Tutu[3]

I can't talk about what anyone has told me in specific detail but I can tell you about my impressions from listening to people make their confessions. Some do it as part of

Christian beliefs about confession

• **Confession gives us the opportunity to be truthful with ourselves.** It helps us to examine ourselves and come face to face with who we are.

• **In the sacrament of reconciliation God gives us a fresh start.** God is a loving heavenly father who knows what we are really like, the good things and the bad things about us. God does not reject us because we have bad points but wants us to come back to him. "While we still were sinners Christ died for us" (Romans 5:8).

• **God is a loving father who actively waits to welcome back his children** who have turned away from him. This is the meaning of the parable of the Prodigal Son (Luke 15), where the father in the story (representing God) is looking out for his wayward son when he finally comes home.

• **God forgives us, whatever we have done.** Some people dread confession and this fear prevents them from going. But we believe that God forgives all sins so long as they are sincerely confessed (1 John 1:9).

• **Confession is about holiness.** The aim of the Christian life is to become holy, like God. However, through sin we often fall away from God's will. In confession we are given a new start. God gives us the Holy Spirit to help us to start again and to become a new creation. In this sacrament God comes to heal people. God says: *I love you. You are accepted, wanted, and loved. Go and sin no more.*

Because people receive God's forgiveness in the sacrament of reconciliation they should go out seeking to be reconcilers—to offer forgiveness to others.

"spiritual direction:" They want to keep on developing, to become more mature as people, and don't want their sins to get in the way of that. Others—I think the majority—come to off-load a real burden, something that just stops them from moving on.

A parish priest

God wants people to turn away from their wrongdoing and to start again. Like the father in Jesus' parable of the Prodigal Son, God is not interested in punishing people but rather in giving them a fresh start.

Confession is about growth

We are often nervous of revealing what we truly feel or what we have done. We fear that other people won't accept us. This is particularly true for young people who are subject to intense peer pressure.

Many people find the absolute confidentiality of talking to a priest helpful. It allows them to open up without fear of rejection or judgment. This may happen informally but on some occasions, it might be helpful to take the step of making a formal confession—with the intention of leaving behind what is troubling. This can lead to personal growth.

The sacrament of confession gives us the opportunity to open ourselves up fully to God. This may take some courage, particularly the first time that we make confession, but without such honesty people do not grow. We should see confession as a time when God takes our secrets in gentle hands, looks upon us with compassion and understanding, and offers us a new start.

To prepare for confession, we should spend time reflecting on ourselves and seeking out our motives. It is only by being reflective and getting to know our weaknesses that we come to understand them. However, we may find it difficult to identify our weaknesses and bring them into the light on our own. This is where a perceptive confessor can help us. Confession then becomes an occasion when we not only receive God's forgiveness but also develop a greater insight into our weaknesses and strengths. It is an opportunity to understand ourselves better.

We often only half know our weaknesses. As a confessor, I try to help penitents reflect on their lives and behaviour. What they only half grasp can become much clearer with the help of a detached, compassionate observer.

A parish priest

During the sacrament of reconciliation, the priest declares Christ's forgiveness to us in a personal way.

Thinking it through

- Imagine that you are standing in front of a secret mirror. Instead of reflecting what you look like on the outside, this mirror is able to reflect what is happening on the inside—it shows you your secret thoughts and feelings. Write down what this mirror would be telling you about yourself right now. You will need to give yourself some time to relax and really examine yourself. You may find the following headings helpful:

  Things I like about myself—thoughts and feelings

  Things I would like to change about myself—thoughts and feelings

- Christians hold differing opinions about confession. Here are two:

  Opinion 1: "When I have done something wrong. I sit down by myself and ask God to forgive me. I do not need to go to a priest for confession—it is God I need to seek forgiveness from."

  Opinion 2: "I think it is important to publicly confess your sins in front of a priest. First, the priest represents God, and it is important to hear God's forgiveness. Second, when we sin we not only hurt ourselves and God but we also affect other people. The priest acts as a representative for other people."

Discuss both these views.

FOR PRAYER & REFLECTION

Most merciful God,
*   we confess that we have sinned*
*   against you*
*   in thought, word, and deed,*
*   by what we have done,*
*   and by what we have left undone.*
We have not loved you with
*   our whole heart;*
*   we have not loved our neighbors*
*   as ourselves*
We are truly sorry and we humbly repent.
For the sake of your Son Jesus Christ,
*   have mercy on us and forgive us;*
*   that we may delight in your will,*
*   and walk in your ways,*
*   to the glory of your Name.*
Amen.[4]

Bible Study

Read Jesus' parable about the Prodigal Son (Luke 15:11-32).

A father has two sons. The younger asks for his share of his inheritance to spend now. He leaves home and spends all the money on wild living. When he has nothing left he decides to return to his father.

- Why did the son decide to return to his father? What do you think was going through his mind?

- What had the son planned to tell his father on his return? What do you think he meant by these words (verses 18-19)?

- How did the father react when he saw his son returning home? Do you think the son expected this reception (verse 20)?

- Why do you think the father arranged for a feast to greet the son? What do you think the younger son would have felt about this? What do you think of the elder son's reaction?

This story is a good example of the process of reconciliation that is at the heart of the sacrament of confession. It is not just a matter of saying sorry—it is a whole process of rebuilding relationships that have broken. The younger son thinks about his actions (*examination of conscience*), realizes that he has wronged his father (*contrition*), goes to *confess* to his father, and receives *forgiveness* and *absolution*.

Some prayer topics

Sins against God—where you have left God out of your life.

Sins against other people—where you have hurt them.

Sins against yourself—where you have damaged yourself through your own attitudes and actions.

Sins against the natural world—where you have treated animals badly or been wasteful of the earth's resources and damaged them through pollution.

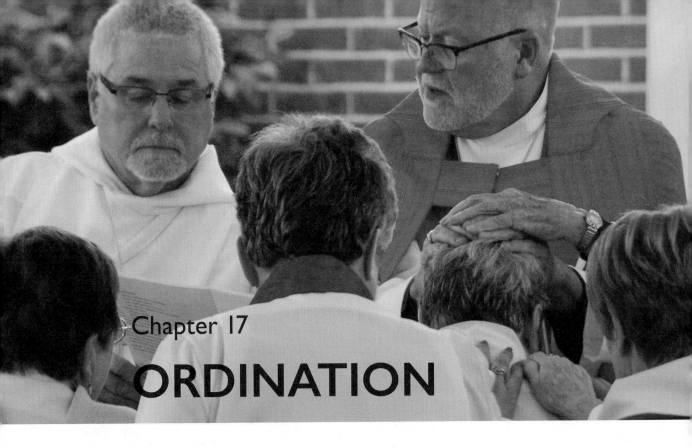

Chapter 17
ORDINATION

If you are still in school, do you have a clear idea of what you want to do when you finish? Some people make up their minds early on and know that they simply must be a mechanic, a teacher, a nurse. Some even feel that they have a calling from God to do a particular task—maybe working for a charity or serving as a missionary in a developing country. The word used for the sense of being called to do something particular in life is *vocation*.

Some people feel that God has called them to be part of the ordained ministry of the Church as a deacon, priest, or bishop. Ordained ministers are called to serve the people under their charge. The importance of this aspect of the priesthood was stressed by Jesus (Matthew 20:25-28). The true follower of Christ must be the servant of others.

A calling

The Holy Scriptures and ancient Christian writers make it clear that from the apostles' time, there have been different ministries within the Church. In particular, since the time of the New Testament, three distinct orders of ordained ministers have been characteristic of Christ's holy catholic Church. First, there is the order of bishops who carry on the apostolic work of leading, supervising, and uniting the Church. Secondly, associated with them are the presbyters, or ordained elders, in subsequent times generally known as priests. Together with the bishops, they take part in the governance of the Church, in the carrying out of its missionary and pastoral work, and in the preaching of the Word of God and administering his holy Sacraments. Thirdly, there are deacons

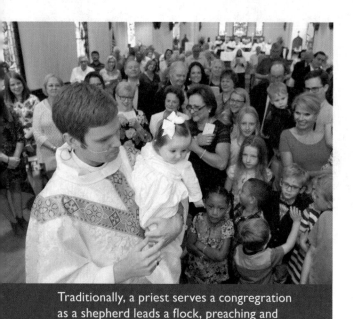

Traditionally, a priest serves a congregration as a shepherd leads a flock, preaching and administering the sacraments.

who assist bishops and priests in all of this work. It is also a special responsibility of deacons to minister in Christ's name to the poor, the sick, the suffering, and the helpless.[1]

Michael Ramsey, who was Archbishop of Canterbury from 1961 to 1974, gave a series of talks to those about to be ordained. These were so influential that they were subsequently published as a book, *The Christian Priest Today*, which is often used by those preparing for ordination. (At the time, only men were ordained, a fact reflected in the language used in the extract, although the advice given has proven to be

Bishops, priests, and deacons: duties and symbols of office

Bishops

Responsibilities: The role of bishops is to oversee the Church, to have responsibility for protecting the gospel, to ensure correct teaching, and to be a focus for the unity of the Church. They are responsible for what goes on in their dioceses. Although there can be only one diocesan bishop, he or she may be assisted by suffragan (assistant) bishops. Bishops ordain new bishops, priests, and deacons, and preside at confirmations and (when present) at eucharists.

Symbols of office: The symbols of a bishop are:

the mitre—its shape symbolizes the tongues of fire of the Holy Spirit, which came down on the multitude at Pentecost;

the staff—it is shaped like a shepherd's crook to show that the bishop is the chief shepherd in the diocese;

a ring—symbolizes that the bishop is wedded to the diocese.

Priests

The word priest comes from the Greek word for "presbyter" (i.e. "elder" in the New Testament).

Responsibilities: The priest looks after a congregation on behalf of the bishop and is sometimes assisted by curates. The priest has three main functions in the local church:

1 to preach the gospel;

2 to administer the sacraments (especially the eucharist), except confirmation and ordination;

3 to exercise leadership—priests share with the bishop in the office of Christ as leader and shepherd.

valuable for both men and women of later generations.)

> While all the people participate, the priest acts in the name of Jesus in the words and actions of the Last Supper...So, too, the other parts of his ministry are in Christ's name: his preaching, his absolving, his caring for people in every kind of way, and his witness to the community.

> Scenes of the mission of Jesus in Galilee and Judaea are reflected in the ups and downs of his ministry...While [the priest] is called to bring the expertise and authority of his ordination into this scene, he knows that expertise and authority are rooted in the humility of Christ.[2]

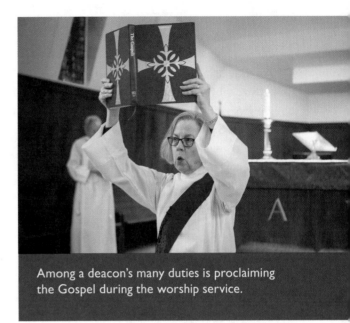

Among a deacon's many duties is proclaiming the Gospel during the worship service.

Through the sacraments, priests mediate (provide a channel for) the salvation Jesus brings to us.

Symbol of office: a long scarf called the stole, which is worn over both shoulders.

Deacons

Deacons provide the foundation for the work of both priests and bishops. The Greek word *diakonos* means servant. The office of deacon originates from the seven men of good reputation who were chosen in Acts to serve others by distributing alms (practical help to those in need) to free the apostles for other kinds of work.

While many deacons continue in this role for their entire vocational life, sometimes the role of the deacon is a last step before becoming a priest. Such people normally spend a year working closely under the supervision of a priest responsible for their training.

Responsibilities: Deacons look after people's welfare, for example, by visiting older people and the lonely, but also by making the whole church aware of such people's needs. Just as Jesus had to be born on earth and live among people before he could bring them to salvation, so the deacon's work is to make Christ present in the community (to "incarnate" him).

In such a way, the deacon prepares the ground for the priest's work of celebrating the sacraments, through which Christ's salvation is brought to us. In worship, the deacon also has the distinctive roles of reading the Gospel and collecting together the people's intercessions (prayers) for common use.

Deacons can carry out baptisms, witness marriages, take communion to the sick, conduct funeral services, and teach and preach.

Symbol of office: a stole worn diagonally over one shoulder only.

Christian beliefs about ordination

- All Christians share in the royal priesthood of Christ: We are all called to live lives of service, praising and thanking God and interceding with God for others. However, some men and women are set apart by the Sacrament of Holy Orders to serve Christ and the Church in this particular way.

- Jesus set apart certain people to preach, heal, teach, and forgive sins, and to exercise authority in the Church. Jesus chose apostles for this task. As the Church spread, the leadership of the Church developed. In the second century, leadership was developed by means of the threefold ministry of bishops, priests, and deacons (see also Chapter 6). This is still the structure of ministry in the Episcopal Church today.

- Bishops are regarded as the direct successors of the apostles. As such, they ordain men and women to be deacons and priests, and they themselves are usually ordained by the presiding bishop and/or other bishops. Ordination usually takes place in the cathedral of the diocese (where the bishop has a seat, *cathedra*).

Thinking it through

- Do you feel that you have a vocation for a particular job in life?

- Discuss with your priest when he or she felt a vocation to the priesthood. How did your priest hear God's call?

- Women were first ordained priests in the Episcopal Church in 1976, and the first woman was ordained a bishop in 1989. However, in other Anglican Communion churches, there is still considerable debate about whether women should be ordained priests and/ or bishops. Why do you think there has been a debate and what do you think are the issues involved?

FOR PRAYER & REFLECTION

*Almighty and everlasting God,
from whom cometh every
good and perfect gift:
Send down upon our bishops, and
other clergy, and upon the
congregations committed to their
charge, the healthful Spirit of thy grace;
and, that they may truly please thee,
pour upon them the continual dew of
thy blessing.
Grant this, O Lord, for the honor of our
Advocate and Mediator, Jesus Christ.
Amen.*[3]

Bible Study

Read Paul's advice to the Roman Church (Romans 12:1-12).

Although this is one of the suggested biblical passages to be read during the ceremony for the ordination of deacons, its content applies to us all.

- What do you think it means to "present your bodies as a living sacrifice, holy and acceptable to God" (verse 1)? Obviously Paul is not advocating physical human sacrifice.

- As Christians we are not to "be conformed to this world" (verse 2). What do you think Paul means by being conformed to this world?

- We are to have a right mind—a right way of thinking (verse 2). You sometimes hear people say, "I can't change, I was made this way!" Here Paul is saying that God can change the way you think and feel for the better. What qualities do you think Paul is talking about here (verse 3)?

- Paul compares the Christian body to a human body which has many parts but works together. He does this to suggest that we all have different gifts which we need to use for one another's good. Which gifts does he name (verses 5-8)?

- Do you think that you have a particular gift for ministry to people?

Some prayer **topics**

For your priest.

For your bishop.

For people training for the priesthood and diaconate.

That each one of us may hear God's call in our lives and that we may have the willingness to listen to God, and obey.

Chapter 18
ANOINTING the SICK

Are any among you sick? They should call for the elders of the church and have them pray over them, anointing them with oil in the name of the Lord. The prayer of faith will save the sick, and the Lord will raise them up; and anyone who has committed sins will be forgiven.

— James 5:14-15

Have you ever been really ill? What did it feel like? It can be a frightening time when you don't understand what is happening to your body. It is easy to feel alone when you are ill, especially when everyone around you seems to be well and living life normally.

Imagine being ill during Jesus' time. There were few effective medicines, and most people lived short lives, blighted by diseases that would be easily treated in a developed country today.

Jesus came to restore people to full health. In the gospels, we read that "the blind receive their sight, the lame walk, the lepers are cleansed, the deaf hear" (Matthew 11:5). This fulfilled the expectation people had about what would happen when the Messiah came. Jesus' healing of people pointed to his nature as Messiah and God's Son.

But Jesus not only healed; he also knew the extremes of physical suffering that human beings can experience through what happened to him when he was scourged and then crucified. Jesus understands human suffering.

In the sacrament of unction (otherwise referred to as anointing of the sick), Jesus comes close to people in their suffering and gives them the power of the Holy Spirit to help them have courage and to take away their fear.

I have anointed a wide variety of people. Sometimes, someone is preparing for surgery and they want to be anointed and prayed with beforehand. On another occasion, I was with a man who had only a few days to live and the anointing brought him immediate peace—it was extraordinary how this happened the moment I anointed him. If you hadn't been there, you might find it difficult to believe the change that happened. I've also anointed someone in intensive care who wasn't expected to survive. Her cousin, a doctor who was there with me when I anointed her, told me afterwards that the turning point appeared to have been the time at which she was anointed. Of course, you can't "prove" this but experiencing this kind of thing has certainly made me more aware of God's Holy Spirit at work.

A priest

This 1940 illustration by a Chilean artist is entitled, "Jesús sana a los enfermos" (Jesus heals the sick). Do you believe Jesus heals the sick? Have you experienced miraculous healing in your life or with a family member or friend?

What happens at the anointing of the sick?

- This sacrament may be requested by those who are seriously ill but also by those who seek a greater mental or spiritual wholeness.

- The priest may be accompanied by family, friends, and members of the sick person's church.

- Prayers are offered for all those who are sick and for the person receiving the sacrament.

- The priest lays hands on the sick person in silence. This is to repeat Jesus' actions when he healed people (for example, see Mark 8:22-26).

- The sick person is anointed with oil on the forehead and the hands as the priest prays for him or her (see the "Prayer for the anointing of the sick" on the following page). Like the oil used at baptism, oil for the sick is blessed by the bishop at a special service usually held during Holy Week.

- Everyone present says the Lord's Prayer. Bread and wine brought from the eucharist may also be given.

- The priest says a final prayer and a blessing.

Why does the priest lay hands on the sick?

There are a number of reasons:

- Jesus sent out his apostles to anoint the sick and heal them (Mark 6:13).

- Jesus laid his hands on people to bless and heal them: for example, Jesus blessed children in this way and restored sight to the blind man at Bethsaida (Mark 8:22-26).

- This practice continued in the early Church. For example, after Saint Paul had become blind, Ananias laid hands on him and Paul's sight returned (Acts 9:12).

- We believe that God's Holy Spirit is released with the laying on of hands. This does not mean that it is always for physical healing. The Spirit also gives spiritual and emotional healing —Jesus referred to the Spirit as "the Comforter," in the sense of "one who gives strength."

Many congregations hold healing services where the priest anoints people with oil and says special prayers for healing.

Christian beliefs about anointing the sick

- **The sacrament for anointing those who are sick brings God close to us in our suffering.** The power of the Holy Spirit is given to help people find peace and courage and at times physical healing. This sacrament is about God's power to heal, to bring hope out of sorrow, life out of death.

- **The sacrament is biblical.** In the letter of James (see the quotation at the beginning of the chapter), the sick are told to request prayer and anointing.

Prayer for the anointing of the sick

As you are outwardly anointed with this holy oil, so may our heavenly Father grant you the inward anointing of the Holy Spirit.

Of his great mercy, may he forgive you your sins, release you from suffering, and restore you to wholeness and strength.

May he deliver you from all evil, preserve you in all goodness, and bring you to everlasting life; through Jesus Christ our Lord. Amen.[1]

Thinking it through

- What do we mean when we talk about different forms of sickness—physical, emotional, spiritual? Try to give examples of each.

- How do you feel when you are sick? If you are in a group, share your feelings with the other members.

Bible Study

Read the advice given in James 5:14-16.

- What does this passage say about the power of prayer? Do you think God can heal every form of illness?

- James clearly says that praying in faith can heal. What happens, therefore, if someone prays in faith and is not healed?

- What do you think of the following situation? David Watson was a priest in the Church of England until he died of cancer. He prayed for healing but died from the disease. He wrote a book, *Fear No Evil*, in the last few months of his life. In it he says: "I still do not know why God allowed [my cancer], nor does it bother me. But I am beginning to hear what God is saying, and this has been enormously helpful to me. I am content to trust myself to a loving God whose control is ultimate and whose wisdom transcends my own feeble understanding."[2]

FOR PRAYER & REFLECTION

For trust in God

O God, the source of all health: So fill my heart with faith in your love, that with calm expectancy I may make room for your power to possess me, and gracefully accept your healing; through Jesus Christ our Lord. Amen.[3]

In pain

Lord Jesus Christ, by your patience in suffering you hallowed earthly pain and gave us the example of obedience to your Father's will: Be near me in my time of weakness and pain; sustain me by your grace, that my strength and courage may not fail; heal me according to your will; and help me always to believe that what happens to me here is of little account if you hold me in eternal life, my Lord and my God. Amen.[4]

Some prayer **topics**

For all who are sick.

For all people who care for a sick person.

For the bereaved—those who have lost a loved one.

Chapter 19

LIFE after DEATH

*Almighty God, look on this your servant, lying in great weakness,
and comfort him with the promise of life everlasting, given in the
resurrection of your Son Jesus Christ our Lord. Amen.*

—*The Book of Common Prayer*, p. 462

How old were you when you first became aware of death? How did you feel?

Many of us have our first experience of death when we are young—a grandparent dies, a friend is killed in an accident, or a family pet dies.

In one sense, death is a very ordinary experience; it is the one thing we all do. On the other hand, it is something out of the ordinary and dramatic. I remember going to my great-grandmother's funeral when I was ten years old. As we drove through the streets on the way to the church, I couldn't understand why life hadn't come to a standstill. My life had.

I wanted everyone to stop what they were doing—their shopping, going to the hairdresser, etc.—and be still, recognizing the very sad thing that had happened in my life: the death of someone I dearly loved.

How do you think of death: as an enemy to be resisted or as a friend? Death need not be an enemy we have to fight. It might be a release if we are very old and tired or very ill. The knowledge and certainty of our death could even be said to focus our minds about how we are going to live this life.

Since Jesus was raised from the dead and promises those who follow him eternal life, Christians believe that death is not the end but the beginning of a new life with God. Saint Paul compared our dead bodies to seeds. When we plant them in the ground, they look dead but nevertheless they grow into a new plant (1 Corinthians 15:42-44). Those close to death use similar pictures. Garvan Bryne was a twelve-year-old dying from a rare bone marrow disease when he explained to his parents that "Dying is not really dying, it is just like opening an old door into a new room which is heaven...there you will meet the people you knew on earth and I am looking forward to that."

Charles Henry Brent, the Episcopal Church's first missionary bishop of the Philippine Islands, expressed something similar in "The Ship," in which he compared letting someone go at death to watching a beautiful ship pass from this shore to the distant horizon. Once the ship is out of our sight, it is coming home to the shore, which is beyond our sight.

What is dying? I am standing on the sea shore, a ship sails in the morning breeze and starts for the ocean. She is an object of beauty and I stand watching her till at last she fades on the horizon and someone at my side says: "She is gone."

Gone! where? Gone from my sight—that is all. She is just as large in the masts, hull and spars as she was when I saw her, and just as able to bear her load of living freight to its destination.

The diminished size and total loss of sight is in me, not in her, and just at the

Look carefully at this fourteenth-century Italian painting depicting the resurrection. What is happening? Who is Jesus comforting? What is happening in the background?

Christian beliefs about life after death and the Last Judgment

• Death is not the end. Instead it is a calling home to be with God. Death is a gateway through which we must pass to live eternally with God. In raising Jesus from the dead God has shown that death has been conquered. Jesus said: "I am the resurrection and the life. Those who believe in me, even though they die, will live, and everyone who lives and believes in me will never die" (John 11:25-26).

• Jesus will return to earth at the end of time (1 Thessalonians 4:16-18). His coming will be visible and personal (Acts 1:11). His return will be seen by everyone (Matthew 24:30; Revelation 1:7). Jesus will return suddenly like a thief who comes in the night (Matthew 24:42-51). This second coming of Jesus will be a grand supernatural event, accompanied by great power and splendour (Luke 21:27-28). Death will be destroyed and Satan and all powers of evil will be overthrown and done away with for ever.

• Before Jesus' second coming, there will be signs that the end is near: natural disasters (Luke 21:11); cosmic disorder (Luke 21:25); social disorder (2 Timothy 3:1-5; Jude 18); international friction—wars, revolutions, political disturbances (Mark 13:7-8; Luke 21:9-10). Before Jesus returns, a number of "false Christs" will lead people astray (Matthew 24:11-13). Biblical texts such as these have led some people to try to predict when the world will end but orthodox Christian teaching is that no one knows when this will happen.

• When Jesus returns he will judge the world. The final judgment will be the climax of world history (Acts 17:31). People will have to give an account of themselves (Romans 14:12) and will be judged according to their actions (2 Corinthians 5:10)—how they have served others, and in so doing how they have served Jesus (Matthew 25:31-46). Those who reject God will in turn be rejected and punished (2 Thessalonians 1:7-9). The final judgment will right the injustices of history.

• The existence of hell, which represents the state of finally being cut off from God. The Bible describes hell using the image of an everlasting fire (Revelation 20:15). A name used for "hell" in the New Testament is *Gehenna*. This referred to the valley of Hinnom outside Jerusalem, where the city's rubbish was burned.

• When Jesus returns Christians will be raised from the dead (1 Thessalonians 4:16) to enjoy eternal life with God. They will be given a new spiritual body that will be free from pain and sickness (1 Corinthians 15:42-44).

• The existence of heaven. Before Jesus died he promised his disciples that he was going to prepare a place for them—in the many rooms of his Father's house (John 14:1-4). The Bible teaches that the earth will disappear (Revelation 21:1) and there will be a new heaven and earth (the word "heaven" here refers to "sky"). In heaven there is no more sickness and death (Revelation 21:4). God will dwell with his people (Revelation 21:3).

moment when someone at my side says, "she is gone," there are others who are watching her coming, and other voices take up a glad shout: "There she comes!" and that is dying.

Charles Henry Brent[1]

The Last Judgment

Have you ever been in trouble at school and had to stand outside the principal's office? Or have you ever had to speak or perform in front of an audience? What does it feel like? These are examples of occasions when we are subject to judgment, which none of us likes. Christians throughout the ages have reflected on judgment because the Bible teaches that Jesus will return at the end of history to judge all people.

But what images of judgment does the Bible present? They are not primarily of someone accusing and condemning people. Rather, the New Testament portrays God as someone who actively pursues those who have done wrong with the intention of saving them and welcoming them to heaven. In the parable of the Prodigal Son, the father, who represents God, goes out of his way to help the son who has rebelled against him. He runs down the road with outstretched arms to welcome him home. In the same way, Jesus spent much of his time with tax collectors and other sinners, those whom his society judged to be outcasts.

However, in the parable of the Sheep and the Goats (Matthew 25:31-46), Jesus refers to a judgment based on how we have responded to the needs of the

What prayers do you say when someone you care for is dying or has died? Many of the psalms offer comfort and hope in these difficult times.

hungry, the thirsty, those in prison, or those in need of clothing and shelter. All who have responded to such needs have, without realizing it, rendered a service to Jesus as well as to the person in need, and they will be given eternal life. Those who have ignored the needs of others will not.

Christians have to hold these and other pictures in balance: God is forgiving and compassionate but nevertheless condemns evil. We also need to be cautious about imagining that we can know what the life to come will be like. Jesus rebukes those who ask him a question about whether a woman who had been widowed several times would have more than one husband in heaven (Mark 12:18-27). He tells them that heaven is not like that, with the implication that such things are beyond our present understanding.

This is the judgment, that the light has come into the world, and people loved darkness rather than light because their deeds were evil.

John 3:19

Hell

The Bible describes hell in a very pictorial way as a place of everlasting fire and punishment (Revelation 20:15). Many painters throughout history have represented hell in this way. It is also described as "outer darkness" (Matthew 25:30) or "deepest darkness" (Jude 6 and 13). These images of hell try to express

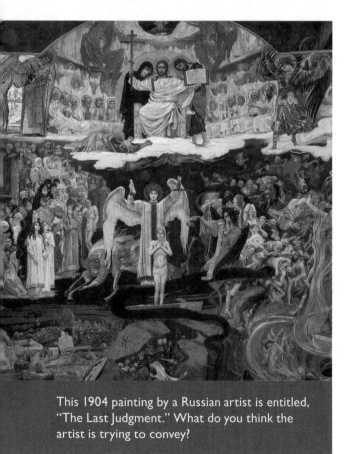

This 1904 painting by a Russian artist is entitled, "The Last Judgment." What do you think the artist is trying to convey?

the state of being far away from God, out of God's loving arms. Such a state of loneliness is torture.

Hell is separation from God, the source of real joy and meaning in life. It is the final "choosing of what is opposed to God so completely and so absolutely that the only end is total non-being."[2]

Some people ask, "How can a loving God condemn people to such everlasting torture?" Christians believe that hell is not simply a punishment: It is something people choose for themselves.

We sometimes use the word "hell" to describe experiences in this life that are completely opposite to God's design for us. Igor Kostin was the first photographer to fly over Chernobyl after the nuclear plant exploded. He has since returned a number of times. His trips have deeply disturbed him. The children he has seen haunt him most: "They are the ones who become innocent victims of our so-called civilization. It's hard to live among normal people now. A person who has been through hell has a different attitude. He breathes the air and feels the sunshine differently."

Heaven

We are not told exactly what will happen to us after death. However, the Bible teaches that when Jesus returns, Christians will be raised from the dead to enjoy eternal life with God.

The Christian hope in heaven is based on what we believe about God's nature. God is immortal (God does not die)—we will have a share in this immortality. God is like a loving father who wants to give good things to his children. God is a just God who will right the evils in the world;

God will judge what is wrong and reward what is right. In the Bible God has promised us life with him for ever. Saint Paul wrote: "I am convinced that neither death, nor life, nor angels, nor rulers, nor things present, nor things to come, nor powers, nor height, nor depth, nor anything else in all creation, will be able to separate us from the love of God in Christ Jesus our Lord" (Romans 8:38-40).

Heaven is not like a reward for doing good deeds. A better analogy is of two people who are engaged to be married. During their engagement they look forward to a time when they can be together. Marriage is a natural extension of their engagement—it is the place to which their love leads them. This is true with heaven, where the Christian's relationship with God leads.

We believe that after death we will be transformed. The life of the caterpillar is a good metaphor. A caterpillar spends most of its life eating, until one day it stops eating and spins a cocoon and turns into a chrysalis. It looks dead. Then a miracle happens: out of the chrysalis a butterfly emerges into a new, free life.

The biblical picture of heaven

The story from John's Gospel of Mary Magdalene discovering the empty tomb on Easter morning is often read at funerals. She goes to the tomb first thing on the Sunday morning after Jesus' death and is horrified to find that his body has disappeared. She fetches some of the male disciples (only men could legally be witnesses then). When they arrive, the Beloved Disciple sees and believes; the rest, including Peter, are still in the dark. They go away and leave her there. She suddenly sees someone she takes to be the gardener and accuses him of taking Jesus' body. Then "the gardener" calls her by name, "Mary," and she knows that it is Jesus. This story shows us two vital things: that Jesus has been raised but also that he has been changed (he is not immediately recognizable). This points us to a recognition that the resurrection is of the person that we know but to a new (changed) life. This means that when you're preaching at a funeral, you hold out to people not the hope of indefinite continuation (which would be awful) but of a new, resurrection life for the person that we have known.

A priest

In the Bible, heaven is described using symbolic language (harps, crowns, gold, etc.). This language is an attempt to describe the inexpressible.

Musical instruments (harps, etc.): Many people associate music with enjoyment. Music creates great pleasure. Heaven is a beautiful place of great pleasure.

Crowns suggest royalty. People go to be with God, who is king of the universe.

Gold suggests the timelessness of heaven (gold does not rust) and the preciousness of it.

Ben Travers, the author of many comic plays, died in 1980, aged 94. In his autobiography he said that he did not desire a tombstone but if he had to have one he would like the following words engraved on it:

This is where the real fun begins.

This sentiment sums up what Christians feel about their life with God in heaven.

The funeral of the reality TV celebrity Jade Goody, who died from cancer aged 27, took place on April 4, 2009. Despite the sadness, the funeral service was a celebration of Jade's life. The message of the funeral service was hopeful: in Jesus we can all experience resurrection and life. The Rev. Corinne Brixton said in her sermon:

We don't expect, do we, to be celebrating a wedding and then to be saying farewell to the bride just six weeks later. She had her fair share, possibly more than her fair share, of life's hardships. But as we've seen, particularly over the past months, she's inspired so many with her courage in fighting cancer and her dignity in facing death. And maybe there's one more thing we don't expect to find as we come to bury this vibrant 27-year-old mother, daughter, wife, and friend—HOPE. Even when we're faced with the harsh reality of death, hope is what is offered by the Christian faith, the Christian faith into which Jade herself was baptised just four weeks ago today. And that hope is found in a living person, Jesus Christ, whose name Jade wasn't afraid to take on her lips: not as a swear word but as the name of the person she wanted Bobby and Freddie to get to know for themselves. I know that Jade liked reading the Gospel of Luke in the New Testament. Why not read it for yourselves? It's interesting that Jade liked Luke's Gospel in particular as it's the one that highlights God's love for unlikely people. She will have read there, in Luke's Gospel, how Jesus welcomed those who weren't particularly religious, and how Jesus spent time with people like herself: down to earth people whose lives, like Jade's, were at times flawed and difficult, but whose lives were precious to God. And she will have read there, in Luke's Gospel, of Jesus bringing the hope that we all need...We don't have a way of finally escaping death, but we do have Jesus, who died for us and then defeated death itself at Easter, giving us hope of life beyond the grave. And that life is not just a continuation of what we have now, but a life that is finally free from sickness, from pain, from grief, and from all that spoils our lives and our world here. How true are Jade's words that heaven is a place where sick people go to be made well, because heaven is where we finally meet face to face Jesus, the greatest healer of all, who alone is able to make our broken lives whole.[3]

Thinking it through

- How does belief in life after death affect the way you live in this life?

- What do you think it means to live your life by the Latin motto *carpe diem* ("seize the day")?

- Consider consciously going through the day's activities as if it were the day Jesus was returning to earth. How would you react differently? What would remain the same?

- C. S. Lewis used to refer to this earthly life as "Shadowlands" in comparison with the afterlife. Why do you think he used this word? Do you agree with this description?

- How would you respond to a person who said, "Although I believe in God and heaven, I cannot believe in hell?"

- The issue of judgment, of heaven and hell, has engaged the minds of many Christian thinkers. Consider the two approaches below and say which one you prefer, and why:

We cannot believe man is free without at the same time believing in the possibility of hell . . . But God does not send people to hell.
Richard Harries,
former Bishop of Oxford[4]

There are only two kinds of people in the end: those who say to God, "Thy will be done," and those to whom God says, in the end, "Thy will be done." All that are in Hell choose it.
C. S. Lewis, *The Great Divorce*[5]

FOR PRAYER & REFLECTION

O God, who by the glorious resurrection
of your Son Jesus Christ
destroyed death and brought life
and immortality to light:
Grant that we, who have been raised with
him, may abide in his presence and
rejoice in the hope of eternal glory;
through Jesus Christ our Lord, to whom,
with you and the Holy Spirit,
be dominion and praise for ever and ever.
Amen.[6]

Bible Study

Read what Paul has to say about life after death in his letter to the Corinthian church (1 Corinthians 15:20-44).

• Why does Paul think that our resurrection from the dead is a certainty (verse 20)?

• How is death described (verse 26)?

• To what does Paul compare the raising of the human body (verses 35-38)?

• How does Paul describe the spiritual body after resurrection (verses 42-44)?

Some prayer topics

Pray for comfort for people who are hurting because a loved one has died.

Ask for courage and a strong faith for those who are dying at this moment.

Thank God for the great hope God has given us that death is not the end.

Ask God for guidance on how best to live this life with one eye on our eternal destiny.

Notes

1 God

1 In J. W. Johnson (ed.), *The Book of American Negro Poetry*, New York: Mariner Books, 1969.
2 Carlo Carretto, *Love is for Living*, New York: Orbis, 1977.
3 James Jones, *Why Do People Suffer?*, Oxford: Lion, 2007.

2 Human nature and sin

1 Fyodor Dostoevsky, *The Brothers Karamazov: A Novel in Four Parts and an Epilogue*, London: Penguin Books, 2003.
2 Adapted from Michael Ramsey, *Introducing the Christian Faith*, London: SCM Press, 1994.
3 William Skidelsky, <guardian.co.uk>, 17 July 2009.
4 Theresa Humphrey, 'Condemned man gives kidney to mother', *San Francisco Chronicle*, 28 April 1995, <http://www.sfgate.com/news/article/Condemned-Man-Gives-Kidney-to-Mother-3035064.php>.
5 *The Book of Common Prayer*, p. 133.

3 Jesus: life and ministry

1 "One Solitary Life," adapted from a sermon by Dr. James Allan Francis in *The Real Jesus and Other Sermons*, Philadelphia, PA: Judson Press, 1926.
2 Robert Van de Weyer in David Self (ed.), *The Assembly Handbook*, Cheltenham: Nelson Thornes Ltd, 1984.
3 Van de Weyer in *The Assembly Handbook*.
4 Charles Colson, *The Body*, Nashville, TN: Thomas Nelson, 1994.
6 David Edwards, *What Anglicans Believe*, London: Mowbray, 1974.

7 C. S. Lewis, *Mere Christianity*, London: HarperCollins, 2001.
8 *The Book of Common Prayer*, p. 213.

4 Jesus: death and resurrection

1 *The Book of Common Prayer*, p. 222.

5 The Holy Spirit

1 Corrie Ten Boom, *Tramp for the Lord: The Years After The Hiding Place*, London: Hodder & Stoughton, 2005.
2 Susan Howatch, *A Question of Integrity*, London: Time Warner, 1998.
3 *The Book of Common Prayer*, p. 227.

6 The Church

1 *The Book of Common Prayer*, p. 329.

7 The creeds

1 *The Book of Common Prayer*, p. 120.
2 Alister McGrath, *Christian Theology: An Introduction*, 5th edn, Chichester: Wiley-Blackwell, 2010.
3 *The Book of Common Prayer*, p. 326-27.
4 *The Book of Common Prayer*, p. 235.

8 The Bible

1 Ernest Gordon, *Miracle on the River Kwai*, London: HarperCollins, 1995.
2 <http://www.bbc.co.uk/religion/religions/christianity/texts/bible.shtml>
3 Sara Miles, *Jesus Freak: Feeding, Healing, Raising the Dead*, Norwich: Canterbury Press, 2010.
4 <http://in.answers.yahoo.com/question/index?qid=20101130104902AA61tc3>
5 *The Book of Common Prayer*, p. 236.

9 Living as a Christian

1 Michel Quoist, *With Open Heart*, Dublin: Gill & Macmillan, 1983.
2 <http://www.npr.org/templates/story/story.php?storyId=91964687>
3 Adapted from Other Prayers, *Common Worship: Daily Prayers*, London: Church House Publishing, 2005, p. 408.

10 Prayer and worship

1 Michael Ramsey, *Be Still and Know*, Eugene, OR: Wipf and Stock, 2012.
2 William Nicholson, *Shadowlands*, London: Samuel French Ltd, 1990.
3 This phrase and those in the subsequent subheadings on p. 66 have their origin in sermons by Michael Ramsey.
4 Carrie Mercier, *Christianity for Today*, Oxford University Press, 1997.
5 *The Book of Common Prayer*, p. 366.
6 From the Collect for the Twelfth Sunday after Trinity, *Common Worship: Services and Prayers for the Church of England*, p. 415.

12 Baptism

1 From *Common Worship: Christian Initiation*, p. 6
2 *The Book of Common Prayer*, p. 302.
3 *The Book of Common Prayer*, p. 302.
4 Open Doors World Watch List 2017.
5 *The Book of Common Prayer*, p. 308.
6 *The Book of Common Prayer*, p. 308.
7 *The Book of Common Prayer*, p. 304-5.
8 *The Book of Common Prayer*, p. 310.

13 Confirmation

1 Montagnard Foundation newsletter, <http://www.montagnard-foundation.org/?p=74>
2 *The Book of Common Prayer*, p. 418.
3 *The Book of Common Prayer*, p. 419.
4 *The Book of Common Prayer*, p. 418-19

14 The Eucharist

1 Adapted from Pierre Lefèvre, *One Hundred Stories to Change Your Life*, Slough: St Paul Publications, 1991.
2 *The Book of Common Prayer*, p. 366.

15 Marriage

1 *The Book of Common Prayer*, p. 427.
2 Adapted from Pierre Lefèvre, *One Hundred Stories to Change Your Life*, Slough: St Paul Publications, 1991.
3 Scott Gunn and Melody Wilson Shobe, *Walk in Love: Episcopal Beliefs & Practices*, Cincinnati, OH: Forward Movement, 2018.
4 *The Book of Common Prayer*, p. 430.

16 Confession

1 Leonardo Boff, *Sacraments of Life, Life of the Sacraments*, Beltsville, MD: Pastoral Press, 1988.
2 *The Book of Common Prayer*, p. 448.
3 <http://www.dadalos.org/int/vorbilder/vorbilder/Tutu/Zitate.htm>
4 *The Book of Common Prayer*, p. 397-98.

17 Ordination

1 *The Book of Common Prayer*, p. 510.
2 Michael Ramsey, *The Christian Priest Today*, London: SPCK, 1985.
3 *The Book of Common Prayer*, p. 817.

18 Anointing the sick

1 *The Book of Common Prayer*, p. 456.
2 David Watson, *Fear No Evil*, London: Hodder & Stoughton, 1984.
3 *The Book of Common Prayer*, p. 461.
4 *The Book of Common Prayer*, p. 461.

19 Life after death

1 From *Favourite Prayers*, compiled by Deborah Cassidi, London: Cassell, 1998.
2 Doctrine Commission of the Church of England, *The Mystery of Salvation*, a report published in 1995.
3 <http://www.chelmsford.anglican.org/jade-goodys-life-celebrated-at-buckhurst-hill-church.html>
4 Richard Harries, *Being a Christian*, London: Mowbray, 1981.
5 C. S. Lewis, *The Great Divorce*, London: HarperCollins, 2009.
6 *The Book of Common Prayer*, p. 223.

Photo acknowledgments

The publisher would like to thank the following for permission to use photographs:

p. 2, 8: Carl Davaz/St. Mary's Episcopal Church, Eugene, Oregon

p. 11: Ggia [CC BY-SA 4.0 (https://creativecommons.org/licenses/by-sa/4.0)], from Wikimedia Commons

p. 17: Miko Stavrev [CC BY 3.0 (https://creativecommons.org/licenses/by/3.0)], from Wikimedia Commons

p. 20: I, JoJan [CC BY-SA 3.0 (http://creativecommons.org/licenses/by-sa/3.0/)]

p. 21: St. Thomas Episcopal Church, Washington, D.C.

p. 22: Contemporary Icon collection, "Christ Sees in the Trinity," 8.5" x 11" egg tempera. Originals by Mary Jane Miller, San Miguel Allende, Mexico, website: millericons.com

p. 23: Mariordo (Mario Roberto Durán Ortiz) [CC BY-SA 4.0 (https://creativecommons.org/licenses/by-sa/4.0)], from Wikimedia Commons

p. 29: A [CC BY-SA 4.0 (https://creativecommons.org/licenses/by-sa/4.0)], via Wikimedia Commons

p. 33: AnonymousUnknown author [Public domain], via Wikimedia Commons

p. 38: St. Peter's Episcopal Church, Geneva, NY

p. 39: Mary Frances Schjonberg/Episcopal News Service

p. 41: Carl Davaz/St. Mary's Episcopal Church, Eugene, Oregon

p. 42: Lori Korleski Richardson/Episcopal News Service

p. 48: [CC BY-SA 3.0 (https:/creativecommons.org/licenses/by-sa/3.0)], from Wikimedia Commons

p. 53 Carl Davaz/St. Mary's Episcopal Church, Eugene, Oregon

p. 57: By Huynh Cong Ut (also known as Nick Ut) - Widely available; This version available at http://www.elenaphotograph.com/blog/noticia.php?id=36, Fair use, https://en.wikipedia.org/w/index.php?curid=36615211

p. 59: Cam Sanders/Episcopal News Service

p. 60: Elke Wetzig (Elya) [CC BY-SA 3.0 (http://creativecommons.org/licenses/by-sa/3.0/)], from Wikimedia Commons

p. 62: Greg Forsyth/Camp Chickagami/Episcopal Diocese of Eastern Michigan

p. 65: St. Andrew's Episcopal Church, Fort Thomas, Kentucky

p. 67: Mike Patterson/Episcopal News Service

p. 70: Carl Davaz/St. Mary's Episcopal Church, Eugene, Oregon

p. 72: Ed Barels/St. Paul's Episcopal Church, Chattanooga, Tennessee

p. 75: Sarah Bartenstein/St. Stephen's Church, Richmond, Virginia

p. 76: Vincent Quiett/St. Titus' Episcopal Church, Durham, North Carolina

p. 77: St. Andrew's, Fort Thomas, Kentucky

p. 79: Robyn Banks/Calvary Episcopal Church, Memphis, Tennessee

p 80: Wayne Cherry/The Church of the Holy Family in Chapel Hill, North Carolina

p. 82: Briget Ganske/St. Stephen's Episcopal Church, Richmond, Virginia

p. 84: St. Andrew's, Fort Thomas, Kentucky

p. 85, top: Beth Dyess, St.Patrick's Episcopal Church, Mooresville, North Carolina

p. 85, bottom: Carl Davaz/St. Mary's Episcopal Church, Eugene, Oregon

p. 87: Mary Frances Schjonberg/Episcopal News Service

p. 88, top: Carl Davaz/St. Mary's Episcopal Church, Eugene, Oregon

p. 88, bottom: Chad Bowman/St. Matthew's Episcopal Church, Austin, Texas

p. 91: top Ken Garner/Church of the Redeemer, Bryn Mawr, Pennsylvania

p. 91, bottom: Robyn Banks/Calvary Episcopal Church, Memphis, Tennessee

p. 92, top: Christopher Corbin/ Thunderhead Episcopal Camp, Diocese of South Dakota

p. 92: (bottom) Todd R. Dill/St. Margaret's Episcopal Church, Waxhaw, North Carolina

About the Authors

Peter Jackson read theology at Oxford, where he also qualified as a teacher and prepared for ordination. He served in two parishes before becoming chaplain and head of religious studies at Harrow School. He taught General Certificate of Secondary English and A level Religious Studies for twenty years. In addition to having been a GCSE examiner, he has also advised the Qualifications and Curriculum Development Agency, chaired a national religious studies association, and trained teachers for King's College London and the Institute of Education. Since 2003, he has been vicar of Christ Church, Southgate, London, where he has trained newly ordained clergy and prepared adults and young people for confirmation. He is also the author of *Ethics for GCSE* (SPCK, 2011).

Chris Wright has taught extensively in Britain and abroad. He has been a lecturer in religious education at King's College London and a headteacher in three schools in the Middle East and in England. He has published a number of books on the teaching of Christianity to teenagers and young adults, including *Key Christian Beliefs*, *Life Issues*, and *Jesus for Today*. He now works with a large family of Church of England schools.

About Forward Movement

Forward Movement is committed to inspiring disciples and empowering evangelists. Our ministry is lived out by creating resources such as books, small-group studies, apps, and conferences.

Our daily devotional, *Forward Day by Day*, is also available in Spanish (*Adelante Día a Día*) and Braille, online, as a podcast, and as an app for smartphones or tablets. It is mailed to more than fifty countries, and we donate nearly 30,000 copies each quarter to prisons, hospitals, and nursing homes.

We actively seek partners across the church and look for ways to provide resources that inspire and challenge. A ministry of the Episcopal Church for over eighty years, Forward Movement is a nonprofit organization funded by sales of resources and by gifts from generous donors.

To learn more about Forward Movement and our resources, visit www.ForwardMovement.org. We are delighted to be doing this work and invite your prayers and support.